Vintage Wedding Cake Toppers

Penny Henderson

Schiffer Publishing Ltd

4880 Lower Valley Road, Atglen, PA 19310 USA

The cake featured on the front cover is courtesy of The House of Clarendon, Inc. (www.houseofclarendon.com). Antique toppers shown are from the collection of the author.

Copyright © 2005 by Penny Henderson
Library of Congress Control Number: 2004114908

Designed by Mark David Bowyer
Type set in Shelley Allegro BT/Aldine 721 BT

ISBN: 0-7643-2172-2
Printed in China
1 2 3 4

Published by Schiffer Publishing Ltd.
4880 Lower Valley Road
Atglen, PA 19310
Phone: (610) 593-1777; Fax: (610) 593-2002
E-mail: Info@schifferbooks.com

For the largest selection of fine reference books on this and related subjects, please visit our web site at
www.schifferbooks.com
We are always looking for people to write books on new and related subjects. If you have an idea for a book please contact us at the above address.

This book may be purchased from the publisher.
Include $3.95 for shipping.
Please try your bookstore first.
You may write for a free catalog.

In Europe, Schiffer books are distributed by
Bushwood Books
6 Marksbury Ave.
Kew Gardens
Surrey TW9 4JF England
Phone: 44 (0) 20 8392-8585; Fax: 44 (0) 20 8392-9876
E-mail: info@bushwoodbooks.co.uk
Free postage in the U.K., Europe; air mail at cost.

Contents

Dedication 4

Acknowledgments 5

Introduction 6

Chapter One: A Brief History of Wedding Cakes 7

    Royal Wedding Cakes 8

Chapter Two: The Cake Cutting Ceremony 10

Chapter Three: Evaluating Your Cake Topper 11

    Determining Age – The Confusion Begins 11

    Bride and Groom Attire, 1890s-1970s 17

    The Personal Touch 26

    Determining Values 28

    Composition – What Is Your Topper Made Of? 29

    Manufacturers and Their Products 30

Chapter Four: The Wedding Album 32

    Traditional 32

    Military 120

    Kewpies and Cuties 127

    Cherubs, Doves, Bells, and the Unusual 156

    Anniversary 165

    Foreign 171

    Cake and Table Decorations and Party Favors 173

Chapter Five: Wedding Cake Toppers – Present and Future 181

Chapter Six: Preservation Old and New 183

Bibliography 184

Resources 184

The Wedding Limo.

Dedication

I would like to dedicate this book to my husband Rodger, for being my inspiration, my lover and romantic, my best friend and supporter, my everything, and now even my editor.

Also, I dedicate this book to my daughter Tacey, for being the light of my life.

I wish also to dedicate this book to my mother and father, Juel and Dave Preston, who made this all possible. I am sure they would be very proud of me if they were still here. Thank you, Mom and Dad, for being my inspiration.

My parents, David William Preston and Loretta Juel Olson. Married July 8, 1946. Zacatepec, State of Morelos, Mexico.

My daughter and son-in-law, Tacey Lenn Mathis and Don Edward Whitney. Married August 11, 1990. Upland, California. *Courtesy of Don Whitney and Tacey Whitney.*

My paternal grandparents, Ernest John Preston and Hilda Marie Malmberg. Married June 28, 1909. Winnipeg, Manitoba, Canada.

My maternal grandparents, Bennie Carl Olson and Carla Henrietta Miller. Married March 23, 1910. Lethbridge, Alberta, Canada.

Acknowledgments

It really does take a lot of help and encouragement from a lot of different people to put a book together. This book was no exception.

I would like to start by thanking my family, who kept prodding me along to write this book. They gave me total support and encouragement. Rodger, my husband and editor, was the brave soul who sat beside me throughout the whole process telling me "You can do it," not to mention "Get out of my hair" from time to time. Many heartfelt thanks to my daughter, Tacey Whitney, and her husband Don, my favorite "son," for their confidence in me. Thank you to my family in the west, my dear sister-in-law, Rebecca (Becky) Watford, her husband Neil, and daughter Anya. Becky and Neil also contributed their lovely wedding photographs. Thanks y'all. You are all the love and light of my life. You are my heroes.

A big thanks to my best friends who kept encouraging me during my "I'm not going to do it" times: Tina Horton, who has been encouraging me since high school; Elizabeth (Betts) Smith; and my special e-mail friend, Dee Lakes (we will meet someday).

I'd also like to thank my very dear friends Judy Plehinger-Smith, Joy and Gary Barr, and Bill and Eula McIntosh for sharing their wedding pictures. Thank you dear hearts…I love you.

Many thanks to my contributors. Mary Swafford, for sharing some of her wonderful collection of cake toppers as well as her knowledge and encouragement. While sharing her collection, we have become good friends. Thanks to Mary's photographer, Kylie Antolini, who did a wonderful job photographing Mary's collection. Also, a special thank you to my friend Diane Kopperman, for sharing her wedding photograph collection with me and giving me constant encouragement, and who is doing a great job of promoting my book.

I started out by asking some confectionary artists how they would suggest preserving a vintage cake topper made from a food based product, when all of a sudden I found out I was talking to some remarkable artists in their field. This added a "new" chapter in my book, "Wedding Cake Toppers – Present and Future," making it possible for me to share their confections with you. Thank you Geraldine Kidwell, B. Keith Ryder, and Rebecca Sutterby, for your wonderful confectionary contributions, especially during June, your busiest time of the year. Also, thanks to Sam Stringer of Stringer Photography (http://www.stringerphotographyKY.com) for taking the wonderful photographs of Geraldine's confections.

Sibylle Jargstorf helped me identify the beautiful Polish bride and groom cake topper in the Foreign category. Thank you Sibylle, for your help with this identification. I am most appreciative.

I would like to give credit here also to the College for Appraisers (www.collegeforappraisers.com), for the excellent appraisal education I received.

I'd like to give special thanks to author Simon R. Charsley, for writing the best historical document about wedding cakes that has been published, *Wedding Cakes and Cultural History*. It's an extraordinary book. Mr. Charsley has done a lot of documented research that helped in my research about the history of wedding cakes and their cake tops. I applaud you, Mr. Charsley, for a job well done.

Thank you Renee Snow, my lifesaver during the worst time I had while writing this book. My computer went kaput and there was my guardian angel, Renee Snow, President of Capricorn Computer Services (www.ccsvcs.com), to save the day. I had never needed a computer technician until my computer broke down with a horrible virus and there she was bright and early on a Sunday, yes, Sunday morning with tools in hand. Within no time, she had my computer back up and running. She went far above the call of duty and deserves a thank you for her efforts. She saved the day.

Last, but certainly not the least, my editors and "best friends," Nancy Schiffer and Donna Baker. They have been dear, patient editors throughout this whole book writing process. Thank you, Nancy and Donna, I hope we have a winner.

Introduction

For me, the collecting seed was planted when I was a small child. My mother collected anything she could get her hands on that screamed "Oriental," and although our home was decorated sparsely, Oriental figurines were always sitting on the shelves, staring back at me. I was to discover later that my mother was obsessed with the collecting bug. As she got older, she became a packrat and saved anything and everything. Unfortunately, she saved nothing of any great value.

After World War II, my father opened a war surplus store. This venture didn't go over very well because of my father's good nature, but the inventory that was left after he closed the store was his fascination. It was years before he started selling some of his leftover World War II and Korean War surplus items, only to start a new collection of coins, stamps, and collector plates. After twenty-five years, I still have parts of my father's collections, which were left to me after his passing.

My first collection was dolls, and I had to have the very latest. I still have most of the dolls from my childhood. When I married in the late 1960s and started raising a family, my collecting days came to an abrupt halt...until I started collecting "owls" in the 1970s. I simply had to have anything that was associated with this beautiful feathered creature of the night. Then, in the mid 1980s, I started collecting Victoriana. This was a far cry from my owl collection. I loved, and still do love, anything from the Victorian period. However, over time I have scaled down my Victoriana collecting to my primary collection, which will always be a part of my life. This collecting romance is for the little gems we call wedding cake toppers, which all tell a story.

My fascination with these charming items began in 1989. On a shelf in an antiques mall sat a bride and groom wedding cake topper that "talked" to me for days before I purchased the little beauties. My husband and I owned this antiques mall at the time, and, as you might imagine, I was in collector's heaven. As a side note, I'd like to mention that during this period we were very fortunate to meet Dr. David Long and his lovely wife Carolyn, who were both appraisers. They established the College for Appraisers and the Appraisers National Association (ANA) and taught classes in a classroom that we provided for them in our antiques mall. The wealth of information I acquired from attending these classes helped me with the skills necessary to write this book. (For more information, contact the college at 5011 Argosy Avenue, Suite 1, Huntington Beach, California 92649, via phone at 800-332-6411, or via their website at www.collegeforappraisers.com.) With our antiques mall providing a great source of collectibles, I acquired the collecting bug so badly that all my varied collections started taking over my house. When I first saw this cute little chalkware couple, I struggled to keep myself from starting yet another collection...but my resolve did not last long. I finally broke down and bought the little pair – and thus my fascination with "wedding cake toppers" (or should I say my never-ending obsession?) had begun.

When I started collecting cake toppers, they were an untapped collector's item. Dealers didn't realize they had something that anybody would actually want to buy, so prices varied from hardly anything to almost nothing. I haunted flea markets, antiques shops, shows, and auctions. My collection flourished as I acquired magnificent pieces without draining my pocketbook. However, with the new resurgence of "romance," times have changed. Now there is a collecting frenzy, with old and new collectors and brides-to-be showing up in the marketplace. Almost everyone knows that they have something very special, so prices have soared and rare and unusual pieces have become even more difficult to find. The competition is brutal, but occasionally I will find a new piece to add to my collection (which, although I've lost count, now numbers in the four hundred plus range). My love and passion for wedding cake toppers will never end. I truly hope this book will bring you lots of visual joy as well as useful information, and that it will help all collectors, old and new, appreciate these fascinating little darlings as much as I do. Happy Hunting!

Chapter One

A Brief History of Wedding Cakes

The use of wedding cakes has been documented as dating as far back as Roman times, when cakes made of wheat or barley were crumbled over the bride's head. The wedding cake was given to the couple and offered to Jupiter, king of the Roman gods. This ceremony was performed in front of a priest and a flame on the cake was lit. The offering showed that the bride was under the control of the groom and, when the cake was eaten, this meant that the marriage was sealed. After this ceremony, the couple was legally married. The burning signified a very sacred bond and the crumbling of a portion of the cake over the bride's head was a blessing for long life and fertility for the couple. Guests often rushed to eat the crumbs as a sign of good luck for themselves. This tradition has evolved to the present day practice of guests taking home a piece of the wedding cake for good luck.

During Medieval times, wedding guests would bring their own small sweet breads or cakes to the ceremony as a gift for the bride and groom. The cakes were then stacked in a tower, as high as possible, making it difficult for the newlyweds to kiss each other over the top. If the bride and groom *were* able to kiss over the tower, this was thought to symbolize a prosperous life together and the hope of having a large family. A similar custom was adapted by the French and Belgians, with the croquembouche cake becoming their traditional wedding cake. This type of cake is built into a tower shape using pastry puffs. These pastries are filled with cream and coated with a thin crisp crust of hard crack sugar, then the tower is decorated with threads of spun caramelized sugar. The word "croquembouche" literally means to crack in one's mouth.

A French chef was visiting London in the 1660s and observed the cake piling ceremony. Horrified at the careless manner in which the British structured their cakes one on top of another, often to have them fall, he came up with the idea of constructing a multi-tiered cake. The British were appalled by this idea at first, but by the 1700s British bakers were displaying the multi-tiered confections suggested by the French chef in their windows. The French have been credited with the frosting of these tiered cakes as well. As described in this chapter, such tiered cakes didn't become the wedding cake as we know it today until the middle of the nineteenth century, however.

As we move into the nineteenth century, we begin to see wedding cakes evolve into their present day form. Until the middle of that century, there is no documentation that brides' cakes were any different than other cakes of the period. They were possibly larger, but otherwise the same as any other plum cake, or fruitcake, as they are also known. The cakes were round, because they were baked in a hoop, and were probably flat on the top. As we have seen, tiered cakes using mounds of sugar mixture already existed, but they were not yet used in the wedding ceremony. The wedding cakes, or brides' cakes as they were known then, evolved from flat cakes by the sheer desire of the bakers of the period to make better quality, and exceptional cakes. The change came about gradually, but it wasn't long before the single wedding cake became a large cake with more than one tier. The bride's cake was then replaced with the wedding cake as we know it today.

The actual wedding cake was first called a "groom's cake" before it was replaced by the name "bride's cake," which was later changed to "wedding cake." Confusing! Even historians have various opinions on how this all came about. However, I will do my best to make a long story short and hopefully historically correct. In the beginning, the "wedding cake" was a plum cake (also known as a fruitcake) or "black" cake that later became known as the "groom's cake" because of its darkness. In America, a lighter white pound cake was preferred, called a "white cake." White, being a symbol of purity, was associated with the bride, so this lighter white cake became known as the "bride's cake." It is theorized that in the mid 1800s, both cakes were combined into one "wedding cake." The groom's cake – considered the secondary one – was taken off the top tier and either saved for later consumption or passed out in little boxes so guests could take a piece home as a souvenir. Later, the groom's cake was separated from the bride's cake to make two separate cakes. The bride's cake then became the primary cake and was then known as the "wedding cake." Having a groom's cake became passé for a time, but bakers say there is a strong resurgence. This seems a good time to mention a tradition of the time. When the groom's cake was passed out in little boxes, unmarried women guests would take their piece home and put it under their pillow, in hopes that they would dream about their future spouse.

Royal wedding cakes closely resembled the cakes of the future, although larger and much more elaborate. The trend towards "high rise" cakes began with royal weddings. For the wedding of Queen Victoria and Prince Albert in 1840, there was a large plum cake, which was circular. It weighed three hundred pounds and is said to have been three yards in circumference and fourteen inches in depth. The cake was decorated with mounds of sugar sculptures. Smaller cakes were made and distributed to the Queen's friends.

In 1858, for the young Princess Royal's wedding, times had changed. The model for her cake was first exhibited at The Great Exhibition in London in 1851. After the wedding, an article appeared in the *Chester Chronicle*, containing the following description of the cake:

The wedding-cake was between six and seven feet high and was divided from the base to the top into three compartments, all in white. The upper part was formed of a dome of open work, on which rested a crown. Eight columns on a circular plinth supported the dome and enclosed an alter, upon which stood two Cupids holding a medallion, having the profile of the Princess Royal on one side, and that of Prince Frederick William of Prussia on the other. Festoons as jasmine were suspended from the capitals of the columns, and busts of the Queen, the Prince Consort, the Prince of Prussia, and the Princess of Prussia were placed on four equidistant bases, projecting from the plinth. The middle portion contained niches in which were a number [4] of statues, including those of Innocence and Wisdom. These statues were separated by broad buttresses of an ornamental character, the upper parts decorated with festoons of orange blossoms and silver leaves. The side of the cake itself displayed the arms of Great Britain and Prussia, placed alternately on panels of white satin, and between each coat of arms was a medallion of the Princess Royal and Prince Frederick William encircled by orange blossoms, and surmounted by an imperial crown. Rows of pearls bordered each division of the cake, which was made by M. Pagniez, Her Majesty's confectioner. The cake was divided into a certain number of portions of slices, and each portion was decorated with a medallion of the royal bride and groom.

The tiers on this cake were not separate cakes. Only the base was made with cake mixture, while the upper tiers were made entirely of sugar. This model was used as well for the official cakes made for each of the Princess's younger siblings.

With each royal wedding, the cakes got more elaborate. All of the official wedding cakes were to include the official cake along with a secondary cake that was more in the form of wedding cakes being used in society at that time. A description of the second cake for the wedding of the Prince Of Wales, as published in *The Illustrated London News* in 1863, read as follows:

It weighed about 80 pounds, and formed an octagon, covered with white satin, each side displaying alternatively medallions of the Prince of Wales, the arms of Great Britain, medallions of Princess Alexandra [the bride], and the arms of Denmark [where she was from]. The cornice was formed of large pearls. The cake was decorated with orange-blossoms and jasmine, and the top was surmounted by a vase filled with a jasmine bouquet.

This would have been different than the cakes we see today, in that the shape was still an enormous version of the single cake with a vase of flowers at the top.

For the wedding of Princess Louise, eight years later, two tiers of cake with a third sugar tier above had become acceptable. The following description appeared in the *Chester Chronicle* in 1871:

It was made in three tiers, placed on a gold stand, weighing about 2 cwt, and measuring at the base of the lower cake two feet in diameter, and in height nearly five feet. The gold plateau had the royal arms on, at for equal distances, with cupids and flowers. The lower tier was ornamented with blue panels, baskets of flowers, fruit, and lovebirds between a scroll leaf, with medallions, containing likenesses of the Marquis of Lorne and the Princess Louise, with their respective coronets above each. The second tier was festooned with the rose, shamrock, and thistle. The third tier was entirely of net work, presenting a very light appearance, with cornucopias and shields, on which were the monograms of the bride and bridegroom. The whole was surmounted by a handsome vase of flowers, with silk banners edged with silver fringe, containing the armorial bearings of the Princess and of the Marquis. Each tier of the cake was bordered with trellise work studded with pearls.

As mentioned earlier, most cakes of this period were baked using a metal hoop. Change came about slowly in the development of how such a large wedding cake could be baked. Many bakers from as far back as 1862 until 1894 had variations on how to bake such a large cake. The ideas ranged from baking the cake in segments that could be fitted together before icing, to putting a pipe or funnel into the center, to the more reliable way of sending the cake to a baker's oven. The consensus was that to bake anything so large in a mould was impractical.

As you can see, it took a lot of sugar paste to achieve the heights that would have been available only to the wealthiest. Another idea for raising the cake's height was to set the cake on a tall stand. Finally, the new technique of tiering in progressively smaller cakes, one on top of another, seemed to be a solution for making cakes rise in height without using all that sugar work, which was cost prohibitive for the masses.

The royal wedding cakes continued to be the grand examples of the period. At the marriage of Prince Leopold in 1882, all three tiers on the cake were made of cake mixture. Eleven years later, in 1893, the Duke of York (later King George V) had a wedding cake with four tiers of cake, plus flowers on top. This cake appeared as an illustration in the *London News* and was modeled and subsequently displayed at the second Annual Confectioners and Bakers Exhibition held in London in September 1894. You can see a picture of this cake in a book titled *Romantic Victorian Weddings Then & Now* (St. Marie & Flaherty, 1992, 58). You just can't imagine all the excessive ornamentation on these cakes until you see one. It's amazing!

By the 1890s, the age of the wedding cake, as we know it, had begun. The cakes were not as grand as the royal cakes, of course, but were nevertheless elaborately adorned with flowers, symbols of love, plus the soon-to-become-popular bride and groom cake toppers that could be removed from the wedding cake and kept as a keepsake for the ages.

Chapter Two
The Cake Cutting Ceremony

The cake cutting ceremony has had several meanings over time, with its evolution no doubt related to the changing role of women in marriage. In earlier times, it was the duty of the bride to cut the cake, which signified leaving behind her old way of life to begin a new life with her new husband. In the early part of the twentieth century, a major change took place in the cake cutting ceremony – it now became the first united act between the newly married husband and wife. The bride normally cuts two slices with the groom's hand placed over hers. This is thought to represent their shared future together, and that no one or no thing can cut into their eternal happiness. The groom feeds the bride some of the cake first, then the bride feeds the groom. When the cake is distributed amongst the guests it is said that the couple is not only sharing their prosperity with family and friends, but that they are sharing the joy of their glorious wedding day as well. My friends and family were kind enough to share their wedding day photographs with you.

Mr. and Mrs. Bill and Eula McIntosh. Married September 30, 1967. *Courtesy of Bill and Eula McIntosh.*

Raymond and Rebecca Watford. Married August 28, 1971. *Courtesy of Raymond and Rebecca Watford.*

Mr. and Mrs. Charles D. and Judith Plehinger-Smith. Married December 31, 1965. *Courtesy of Judith Plehinger-Smith.*

Chapter Three

Evaluating Your Cake Topper

Determining Age — The Confusion Begins

Determining age can be a difficult task at times. Of course, it would be wonderful to have full written or verbal documentation about a certain cake topper, but it is highly unlikely that you will have this information available to you. My research has found no historical documentation as to when the first bride and groom cake topper was placed on top of a wedding cake. Maybe an inventive baker experimenting with new ideas was the first to use one, or possibly a bride-to-be who wanted to be different. However, we have a good idea when the practice started.

Flowers were the rage throughout the Victorian era. As a result, real and sugar paste flowers were placed all over cakes. By the late 1880s, advertisements in trade catalogs were displaying attachable wedding cake toppers. Artificial flowers were the first arrangements that could be removed by the newlyweds and placed under a dome as a keepsake of their wedding. Most of these new removable toppers consisted of flowers or other symbolic symbols, such as cupids, joined hands, bridal slippers in silver or white, doves on metallic rings, and horseshoes. These ornaments have in fact remained popular on cakes to this day. Then, in 1892, a Scottish firm advertised in the *British Baker* that they were making a bride and groom cake topper using a patented icing powder. The age of the bride and groom cake topper began with a roar, and these toppers became the rage all over the world.

The United States was the forerunner in the production of mass produced bride and groom cake toppers. This suggests that they were made in molds. By the turn of the twentieth century, these little darlings were on top of almost every wedding cake. Toppers were produced with brides and grooms standing under a horseshoe gazebo, with the words "Good Luck" and "Constancy." Another style might display a blacksmith standing amongst flowers forging wedding bands. Each of these toppers stood on an elaborate pedestal (hereafter known as a base) made of a food product. Catalogs from the late 1800s described and/or illustrated bride and groom cake toppers using sugar based materials (hereafter known as food product). These confectioners' catalogs offered the bride an abundance of choices for adorning the top of her cake. Shown here are some examples of these catalogs and illustrations.

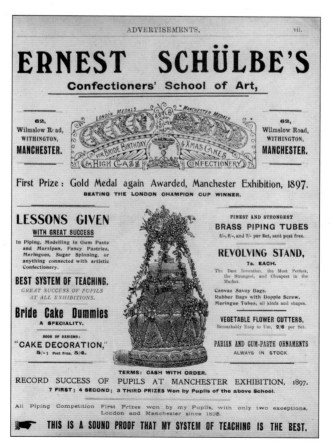

Advertisement for Earnest Schülbe's Confectioners' School of Art. c. 1900.

Title page from *Cake Decoration, Cake Tops, Sides, and Ornaments*, a book by Earnest Schülbe. Dated 1906.

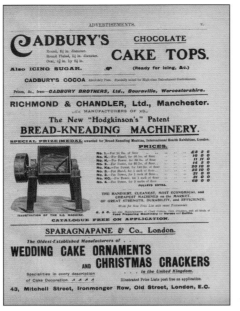

Advertisement for Cadbury's Chocolate Cake Tops and Sparagnapane & Co., London, Wedding Cake Ornaments. c. 1900.

Advertisement for Tom Smith wedding cake toppers made from gum paste. c. 1900.

Advertisement for Tom Smith & Company, Ornamental Confectioners. c. 1900.

Very few cake toppers have the manufacturer's name, patent date, and/or actual manufacturing date stamped or embossed on the base. For all those that are not marked, the most effective way of establishing age is to identify the style of clothing worn by the wedding couple on your cake topper. There were different styles for both men and women, in almost every decade. However, as you will see later in this chapter, some styles run into the next decade, making it somewhat difficult to determine the actual manufactured age of the cake topper.

In addition, I have an example of one cake topper showing the style of costume from the 1930s, but on the bottom of the topper is marked "married in 1948." Another example that I will show you was used on a couple's cake in the 1930s, but again, I feel this topper was made the decade before. A third looks like the couple came right out of a 1940s Humphrey Bogart movie, yet writing on the bottom of the cake topper base indicates it was used on a wedding cake in Palm Springs, California in 1952. So, in a number of cases, when a topper was manufactured and when it was actually used may be quite different. A growing trend now is to reuse our mothers' or grandmothers' wedding cake toppers. Was this trend followed in past times, as well? The confusion never ends.

As mentioned earlier in this chapter, early trade catalogs dating back to the 1890s began showing illustrated examples of cake toppers for sale. An actual picture of an early cake with its topper would have been hard to take, since the cake in most cases would have to be photographed in a studio. I was lucky enough to find a picture that was taken in a studio in Arkansas, showing a proud master baker standing alongside his culinary masterpiece. Another early photograph of a cake topper was taken in a studio in Pottstown, Pennsylvania. The topper appears to be made of food product flowers with what is apparently a real stuffed bird dangling from the center of the topper. I'd like to think the bird was made of spun cotton, but I don't think so.

A baker proudly stands by his confectionary creation. c. 1900.

A picture of an early cake topper displaying a bird as the centerpiece. c. 1900.

Prior to the 1940s, a majority of cake topper bases being produced were made of a sugar food product. In the 1940s, this practice began to change due to the rationing of sugar during World War II. The composition of the majority of bases as well as of the brides and grooms would eventually be plaster of Paris, hereafter known as chalkware. I suspect there was a time period during World War II in which cake toppers were not being produced; I will go into more detail about this in the next paragraph. The war rationing prevented many couples from being able to have a wedding cake. Those lucky couples who did manage to have a cake were able to do so because family and friends would pool their ration stamps to help provide the rationed materials necessary to have the cake made. It is interesting to note that in the late 1940s, following the restricted use of wedding cakes during the war years, cakes were becoming the centerpiece of the wedding ceremony once again. The tiers on wedding cakes were built so high that the bride and groom could hardly be seen standing behind them.

To add to the confusion factor, I found during my research for this book that there seems to have been little or no productivity in the manufacture of bride and groom cake toppers during the World War II years, 1939 to 1945 (both here and in England, as well as Japan and Germany). We know that there was a rationing on the use of sugar and plastic based products during this period, and imports from Japan and Germany had ceased. In researching this period, I have found that my dated chalkware cake toppers from the 1940s were made after the war years. The chalk or chalkware figures before that period are undated and appear to have been made either as separate figures or attached figures made in the 1930s, due to the style of the brides' attire. Were couples using leftover cake toppers from an earlier period during the war years? If so, does this mean that there was relatively little or no production of cake toppers during World War II? It appears to look this way. These figures resemble their 1930s bisque counterparts in almost every detail except for examples where the groom is a uniformed soldier. However, there are written wedding dates on the bottom of some of these toppers with early 1940 dates. I will continue my research in this area in hopes of finding the answer to this riddle. Until the answer is found, however, the bride and groom cake toppers of this period that I have just described will be identified with a circa date of 1930/1940.

Composition is another clue to age. Food products were used in the early manufacture of these treasures. This was followed by porcelain, bisque, celluloid, papier mâché, crepe paper, and pipe cleaner. The 1940s brought in the era of mass produced chalkware. However, many of the compositions from the earlier decades were also used during this era. Chalkware seemed to prevail until the late 1950s, when plastic became not only the norm but was being mass produced.

To be more precise about composition, from the late 1800s through the 1930s and early 1940s, a food product was normally used for the base. From the late 1800s to the early part of the 1900s, even the bride and groom were made of a food product. Through the 1920s and into the 1930s, you might still find the bride and groom made of a food product. However, during the 1920s and through the 1930s, non-food products (i.e., celluloid, papier mâché, bisque, etc.) were also used for the bride and groom. In the 1940s and 1950s, both bride and groom were usually made out of chalkware. However, you will also find examples of a new form of plastic, due to the new technique of plastic injection molding being produced in the late 1930s to the early 1940s. This technique appears to have ceased during the World War II years and was revived again using a similar technique in the 1950s. In the 1950s through the 1970s, both bride and groom were plastic; however, a bisque or porcelain bride and groom was occasionally added. Keep in mind that while this is a good guide to follow, it is not exact. As mentioned earlier, some materials and products overlapped from one decade to the next.

For identification purposes, the early plastic examples appear to be thicker and heavier than the later examples produced in the 1950s and 1960s. Another clue to help with age identification is the "taste test" – this can help determine if the wedding couple or base are either chalkware, bisque, or a food product. If you gently touch your tongue against the item in question you may get a sweet taste; if not sweet, then it is chalkware, or possibly bisque. If you do find that the topper is made from a sugar food product, as a rule of thumb it will normally be older than the chalkware or bisque product. Here again, more confusion, however. Manufacturers were once again using food products in the 1950s, so you'll have to get a feel of what the style is, as well as the composition of your topper, to date it.

Cake toppers other than a bride and groom are timeless. These would include cherubs, clasped hands, horseshoes, slippers, shoes, cupids, Kewpies, bells, doves, and wedding bands. Examples of these have been found in various compositions, as you will see, and composition is the one of the best ways of determining their age. Sometimes style can be used in addition. For example, wax clasped hands can be dated to the early 1900s and throughout the 1920s because of their popularity during this period. (They might even go as far back as the late 1800s, but to date, I haven't found that to be fact.) Kewpies date to the late 1910s, because that is when Rose O'Neill invented them and went to Germany to have them made. They were made of many different compositions throughout their popularity into the 1940s. "Wedding chapel bells" have appeared on wedding cakes since the very first wedding cakes were made and are still being used today. Doves and cherubs would also fall into this category. So, as you can see, the best way to determine age of these types of toppers is by composition and style. They can be made of anything from spun cotton, food products, chalkware, bisque, celluloid, porcelain, and mercury glass to plastic and probably other things yet to be discovered. Knowing what the item is made of and when the style was popular will help you determine the age of your cake topper.

For the Kewpie bride and groom, the category is endless. As noted above, Rose O'Neill was the artist who created these cute little dimpled children. Just before World War I, Kewpies were being imported from Germany in the form of bisque. During the war, however, shipping embargos ended the imports from Germany. The United States continued to make Kewpies in bisque, and also added wood pulp, chalk, and celluloid to the materials being used. Kewpie cake toppers started appearing on cakes in the late 1910s and into the 1940s, with new bisque styles still seen on cakes today. With the exception of the newer bisque Kewpies, all previously mentioned toppers were similar in style and materials. Not an easy task to date, as you can see. But hopefully I have given enough age clue identifiers to help you determine the era in which these pieces were manufactured.

From the 1880s until World War II in Britain and Scotland, silk or paper banners with the initials of the couple and the date of the wedding were popular and would be hung from a rod or stick and placed above or beside the cake. You will see an example of one such pair in The Wedding Album, under the Foreign category on page 173.

Another observation is early examples of bride and groom cake toppers were standing separate from each other. I have found no documentation as to why this happened, but I suspect it might have been because they either found them easier to mold them separately, using food product, or because of the strict social etiquette rules of the 1890s and the early 1900s

In my research of bisque German figures, I was unable to verify the marks on the figurines that have only "Germany" incised or stamped on the bottom or back of the figures. Some of these also have numbers that I believe were mold identification marks. Since I was unable to identify the marks, I was also unable to confirm the manufacturer or date of manufacture. I found this to be true with most "Japan" marks as well. I have tried to date them as accurately as possible by their style of costume. This was difficult at times, because styles from different periods may appear on the same figure. That is, a bride's gown may have a 1930s bias cut appearance, but the headdress and hairstyle are from the 1920s. Of course, the late 1920s were starting to move into the 1930s fashions. This bit of overlap may add to the confusion.

Due to such overlaps in styles, trends, or the use of older molds, please keep in mind that when I give a circa (c.) date for a figure, that figure may have been used the decade before or the decade after the date given.

Don't be discouraged about dating your cake toppers. With the information I have given you in hand, you should be able to determine the age of your topper within a ten year period. This said, I have done my very best to date and describe the cake toppers in this book accurately, using my appraisal education, lengthy research, and the knowledge I have acquired from years of collecting.

During my photography sessions, I began noticing that despite similarities in so many of my cake toppers, they were still different – they might have the same composition and style but come in different sizes; might have the same style but different composition; might have the same composition and similar style but be made from different molds, etc. I thought it would be interesting to share some of my findings with you.

This example shows you a grouping of similar styles made in different sizes and with different molds. The tall couple in the center was made in Germany while the others were made in Japan. This is also a good example of how the Japanese were trying to imitate the German figurines.

These two toppers are perfect examples of the same bride and groom being used in different periods. The figures on the left are dated 1974 and the base is dated 1959. The figures on the right are also dated 1974 but the base is dated 1980. Both are by Coast Novelty Mfg. Co. This particular bride and groom style was used throughout the 1970s and into the 1980s.

This is one of two examples showing a similar style, period, and size, but different compositions. Here, the figures on the left are chalkware and the figures on the right are made of hard, thick plastic. Both are from the 1940 period.

The example above shows a chalkware couple on the left and a bisque couple on the right. Both are from the 1940s.

In these five examples, the toppers in each photograph are made of the same composition, are the same type of figures, and are from the same period, but in different sizes.

As noted earlier, the foremost way to determine the manufactured age of a bride and groom cake topper is by the style of their wedding attire. However, as I have also mentioned earlier, these styles may at times overlap from one decade into another. Opinions vary among costume historians as to the exact costumes worn for each of the various periods. To help with this major identifier, I have used historical data, period pictures, and my cake toppers to establish a style checklist showing the main style attributes that can be used for identification of a majority of cake toppers. Although proper attire existed for casual, semi-formal, and formal weddings, most bride and groom cake toppers appear to be wearing formal attire; therefore, I will primarily concentrate on the formal wear of the period. I have also added some period style drawings to help with era identification. I hope that this style checklist and the drawings will help in your endeavor to date your cake toppers.

1890 through 1900

Bride

- Bodice and skirt are separate
- Skirt cut narrow over the waist
- Smooth fitting over the hips and hung straight to the floor in front
- Fullness in the back
- Hem touched the floor
- Most of the decoration was on the bodice
- Sleeves became very full and were called "leg of mutton" sleeves
- Later in the decade, sleeves became tighter at the forearm, graduating to a large puffed sleeve on top
- High, close-fitting collars usually covered with lace
- Full length court style trains
- Veil was floor length or longer and attached to the top of the head by gathering and adding a garland of flowers usually made of artificial/wax orange blossoms
- Occasionally, large brimmed hats were worn, but usually only by bridesmaids

Groom

Note: There was a very strict social pecking order of the period. Wealthy men wore a black frock coat, described as a close fitting coat with a square bottom that reached down to the knees. Accessories were black or gray striped straight leg trousers, wing tip or turnover collar and white shirt, gloves, white linen handkerchief, boutonniere, and silk top hat and necktie. A tradesman wore a morning/cutaway coat, described as a long jacket with skirts tapering from the front waistline to form tails at the back. Accessories for a morning coat were straight leg trousers (usually black, sometimes gray stripe), white shirt with a wing tip collar, ascot tie, white double breasted vest, white kid gloves, black or gray striped trousers, white carnation, white linen handkerchief, and black silk top hat. Working men wore a lounge suit. This isn't what it implies, rather it is a business suit that was worn for informal occasions. It was based on the cut of a working man's clothes, but in a lighter weight fabric. The jacket was close fitting with high set lapels and rounded lower front edges. The trousers were straight legged and usually light in color. A shirt and waistcoat were also worn. If they were indeed gentlemen, they would adhere to these strict social rules.

- Black frock coat with accessories (wealthy man)
- Black morning coat with accessories (tradesman)

The following examples show style characteristics found in the 1890s decade.

1890s Bride: High collar covered with lace; narrow waist; smooth hip; fullness in back; wax flower headband; floor length veil.
1890s Groom: Black cutaway jacket; black straight leg trousers; vest or waistcoat; white carnation.

1890s Bride: High collar covered with lace; narrow waist; smooth hip; leg of mutton sleeves with tight forearm; floor length veil; wax flower headband.
1890s Groom: Black lounge suit; turnover collar; black straight leg trousers; black vest or waistcoat; white carnation.

Bride

- Gibson Girl style
- Lighter weight materials used, such as lace, chiffon, or soft velvet
- Fullness changed from backside to bosom
- S-shaped corset thrusted the top half of the body forward. This created a blousy effect at the waist
- Narrow waistline
- High neckline covered with wide band of lace. Depending on social status, some brides chose to wear lower cut, draped necklines.
- Button down back
- Bodice and skirt usually separate
- Skirt flowed over hips
- Sleeves long to cover arms
- Veil and headwear were varied
- Floor length or longer veils held on the head with flowers; also waist length veils were popular
- Veil usually covered hair and framed the face with minimum trim
- Many brides chose to wear hats rather then veils
- Full length court trains
- Walking length skirt
- A very short return of the "leg of mutton" sleeves

Groom

Note: Etiquette was still in place for the social pecking order. Styles had not changed.

- Black frock coat with accessories (wealthy man)
- Black morning coat with accessories (tradesman)

The following examples show style characteristics found in the 1900s decade.

1900s Bride: High, close fitting collar; hat; leg of mutton sleeves; fullness in bosom; flowing hipline.
1900s Groom: Black lounge suit; matching straight leg trousers; black vest or waistcoat; linen handkerchief; boutonniere.

1900s Bride: High, close fitting collar; wax flower headband; long veil; fullness in bosom; narrow waist; flowing hipline; long sleeves and gloves.
1900s Groom: Black lounge suit; matching trousers; black waistcoat or vest; turnover collar; white kid gloves; boutonniere.

Illustration of a Gibson Girl and her dress form, showing the S-curve with the thrusted top half and narrow waistline.

18

Bride

Note: World War I brought about many style changes during this period.

- S-shaped 'Gibson Girl' style disappears
- More relaxed fashion
- Early part of decade waistline became less defined; called "empire" style
- Later part of decade the waistline was defined with a sash
- Light weight materials used, such as chiffons and satin
- Narrow "hobble" skirts that made it difficult for women to walk
- Skirts were overlaid with draped material at the bottom; called the "Harem" skirt
- Exotic influence
- Trains became shorter
- Sleeves were slashed or fitted
- Skirts and bodice crossed in laired fashion
- During the war years, hemlines became short with full tiered skirts
- After the war (1918), hemlines returned to longer slender length once again, but panels and layers were added so walking was made easier

- Cap style veils of net worn with cluster of orange blossoms
- Veils reached to the floor or longer, however some brides chose shorter veils
- Necklines varied from high collar, V-neck, to round neck

Groom

Note: The social pecking order was now more relaxed and by the end of the decade was non-existent.

- Frock coat with accessories until World War I
- Morning coat with accessories
- Black tuxedo/dinner jacket with white pleated formal wing tip collar, white shirt with vest and bow tie, matching trousers, white carnation, and white linen handkerchief
- Black tails, a full dress coat with two long tapering tails at the back. Usually black during this period. Worn with matching trousers of the same color, white shirt with wing tip collar, white bow tie, white single breasted low cut vest, white carnation, white linen handkerchief, silk top hat

The following examples show style characteristics found in the 1910s decade.

1910s Bride: Sash at waist; narrow draped or laired skirt; cap style headpiece with wax orange blossoms; short veil; round neckline.
1910s Groom: Black cutaway jacket; black vest or waistcoat; grey stripe trousers; necktie; linen handkerchief.

1910s Bride: Narrow hobble skirt; fitted sleeves; laired bodice; cap style headpiece with wax orange blossoms; floor length veil; high v-neckline; short train.
1910s Groom: Black tails; black trousers; white shirt vest; wing tip collar; white bow tie; white carnation.

Bride

- Ankle length, natural waist with sash
- "Harem" or draped skirt hemline popular
- Material draped and crossed bodice
- By 1923, hemlines went back up
- Later, waistlines went down to the hips
- By 1925, there was no waistline…the "Flapper Era" began
- Chemise or sheath style dresses
- Sleeves became shorter
- Handkerchief point on hem in the mid-1920s
- Narrow chiffon dresses in the late 1920s
- Loose fitting laired gowns and uneven hems, long and short
- Hair worn short
- Bridal headwear worn in the style of the new cloche hat, close to the head, with a veil
- Veil short or fell to the floor or longer
- By 1928, the figure was starting to show again and the 1930 style was emerging
- Decorated prayer books sometimes carried in place of flowers

Groom

- Very little change from the previous decade
- Frock coat was out of fashion
- Morning coat with accessories
- Black tails with accessories
- Black tuxedo with accessories

The following examples show style characteristics found in the 1920s decade.

1920s Bride: Short sheath style dress; uneven hem; short sleeves; hat.
1920s Groom: Black lounge suit; black trousers; white tie; linen handkerchief; boutonniere.

1920s Bride: Short, narrow chiffon style dress; short sleeves; short hair; close fitting cap; long veil.
1920s Groom: Black tails; black trousers; white shirt and vest; white bow tie; wing tip collar.

Bride
- Statuesque figure and designed to flow with the body in motion
- Fitted and flowing with long sweeping lines
- Hem flared into a mermaid tail
- Hemlines were also ankle length
- Soft materials such as crepe and satin were cut on the cross/bias, so that the material would cling to the shape of the body
- Necklines plunged into V-shaped fronts and dropped dangerously low in back
- Cowl necklines also popular
- Puffed flounces on the shoulders
- Bias cut triangles pieced and sewn together into a one piece dress that would slip over the head and conform to the body without a side or back
- Long fitted sleeves came to a point over the hand
- Headwear was as sleek as the dress, with neatly arranged hairstyles

- Mantilla tiered veil or Juliet tiara style cap with tiered veil falling down the back, away from the face, to the bottom of the gown
- By the late 1930s, light color gowns became popular
- "Leg of mutton" sleeves returned shortly
- Ruffled skirts were taking shape because of the popular movie, *Gone With The Wind*
- Late 1930s fashions turned toward the princess (A-line) style used throughout the 1940s

Groom
- Black tails with accessories (remember Fred Astaire)
- Morning coat (better known as the cutaway by this period) usually worn with striped trousers and accessories

Note: Nearly all of my cake toppers from this period show the groom wearing a long tie, not a bow tie.

The following examples show style characteristics found in the 1930s decade.

1930s Bride: Flowing satin ankle length gown; cowl neckline; puffed flounces on shoulders; long fitted sleeves; floral headband with floor length veil flowing down the back; mermaid tail train.
1930s Groom: Black tails; black trousers; white shirt and vest; wing tip collar; white bow tie.

1930s Bride: Satin fitted and flowing gown; mermaid tail; slim floral headband with very long veil flowing down the back and over the gown.
1930s Groom: Black cutaway jacket; grey stripe trousers; white shirt; wing tip collar; ascot tie; black vest or waistcoat; boutonniere.

21

Bride

- A-line princess style skirt
- Fitted bodice
- Sweetheart neckline
- Peplums, short skirts, or ruffle sewn to the bottom of a bodice
- Long fitted sleeves coming to a point over the hand
- Puffs at the shoulders
- Veils usually to the fingertip or elbow length
- Veil worn with a crowned tiara, tulle, or heart shaped headdress
- Collars off the shoulder, rounded, or V-neck
- Bell shape gowns took shape in the late 1940s and became popular in the 1950s

Note: Even though the style trend during World War II was usually a wedding suit, most cake toppers show the bride wearing a long gown.

Groom

- Cutaway suits with the usual accessories
- Tuxedo with accessories
- Black tails with accessories
- Military men wore their full dress uniforms

The following examples show style characteristics found in the 1940s decade.

1940s Bride: Pink gown; Sweetheart neckline; princess style skirt; puffs at shoulders; long sleeves.
1940s Groom: Naval dress uniform.

1940s Bride: Princess or A-line skirt; fitted bodice; puffed at shoulders; long sleeves; V-neck; cluster of orange blossoms with long flowing veil.
1940s Groom: Black cutaway jacket; black vest or waistcoat; grey stripe trousers; white shirt; wing tip collar; ascot tie; boutonniere.

Bride

- Bell shape silhouette
- Cinched waist
- Rigorous shaping of undergarments to mold the bosom into points and pull the waist in
- Tight fitting bodice covered with lace
- Billowing skirts to emphasize a small waist
- Crinoline skirts held up by petticoats of starched organza and net
- Gowns floor length with or without trains
- Calf length gowns also popular
- Layers of tulle
- Sleeves were long fitted, short cap, or strapless
- Chantilly lace became popular
- Headwear usually small decorated coronets, Juliet caps, and wide bands
- Elbow length veils or shorter were puffy like the dress, and attached to the headpiece
- Collars were rounded, V-neck, off the shoulder, and strapless
- Jackets with "Peter Pan" collars often worn over strapless gowns
- Gowns became sleeveless for the first time since the 1920s

Groom

- Cutaway/morning coat with accessories
- Sometimes a white suit was worn with a Fedora hat
- Tuxedo either black or midnight blue with accessories
- White tuxedo/dinner jacket with midnight blue dress trousers and accessories
- Navy blue tails with accessories

The following examples show style characteristics found in the 1950s decade.

1950s Bride: Soft, bell shape skirt; cinched waist; heart shape headdress with shoulder length veil; chantilly lace over satin; long fitted sleeves; V-neck; small nosegay.
1950s Groom: Black tuxedo; black trousers; wing tip collar; white shirt; white bow tie.

1950s Bride: Full bell shape gown; cinched waist; headband with short veil; chantilly lace over satin; long fitted sleeves.
1950s Groom: Black tuxedo; black trousers; wing tip collar; white shirt; black bow tie; white carnation.

1960 through 1970

Bride

- Waistlines went up and down, as did hemlines
- Early 1960s similar to previous decade
- Fashion became haphazard and not dictated by fashion designers
- Took on a childlike appearance
- The waist dropped and the simple shift style became the rage
- Long trains became an added extension from the skirt and sometime fell from the shoulders
- Waistlines became looser and higher in the style known as empire
- Skirt fullness became stiff or padded
- Front of the skirt was flat, giving way to pleats or gathers
- Fitted bodices were still popular, with fitted sleeves that came down over the hand
- Short bouffant veils were popular, but instead of wearing a cap or hat, the veil was attached to a flower on the top of the head
- Pill box hats with veils also very popular
- Even though dresses were getting shorter, most brides preferred a long wedding gown.
- Toward the end of the 1960s, fashion became nostalgic and Victorian styles with a button down bodice, high collar, and cuffed sleeves were becoming popular
- Lace was becoming more and more popular once again
- The symbol of the period, flowers, was applied to everything from the headdress to the veil and eventually to the dress

Groom

- Lounge suit with a tie
- Cutaway suit with gray trousers and accessories

The following examples show style characteristics found in the 1960s decade.

1960s Bride: Fitted, one piece stiff satin gown; floor length; long fitted sleeves; long veil; floral headpiece.
1960s Groom: Black tuxedo; black trousers; white shirt; black bow tie; boutonniere.

1960s Bride: Red velvet empire style dress; knee length.
1960s Groom: Gray lounge suit; matching trousers; gray vest; boutonniere; notice the thin tie.

1960s Bride: Childlike style gown; cinched waist; Peter Pan collar; long full cuffed sleeve; short bouffant veil; button down front.
1960s Groom: Black lounge suit; matching trousers; gray shirt; black and blue necktie; boutonniere.

24

Bride

- Changes in bridal wear numerous during the 1970s
- Nostalgic, Victorian to medieval style
- High waists (empire) fashionable most of the period
- Princess cut without sleeves
- *Gone with the Wind* style hats in place of veils
- Veils usually elbow length with a Juliet cap when worn
- Floral prints
- Camelot sleeve, which fit like a short sleeve and bloused at the forearm, was worn with a flowing empire style gown
- Full skirts with no hint of a waistline
- Victorian revival, new princess A-line gown with high necks and balloon sleeves
- Nylon or other synthetic sheers
- Floral appliqués at the bust, wrist, and hems
- Dust ruffle hems and ruffle bodice
- Double knit gowns featuring flowing drop backs and batwing sleeves, with an empire gown
- Stretch knit gowns with a circumference of nearly twenty feet
- By the end of the decade, the rage was designer fashions

1970s Bride: Satin princess skirt with laced bodice (medieval flair); mid length veil.
1970s Groom: Tan lounge suit with full (flair) cut jacket; matching flared trousers; tan shirt; carnation.

Groom

For the groom of the 1970s it was also a time of experimentation, within boundaries. The traditional black tails and striped trousers were now the exception rather than the rule. The groom who dared might try a blue worsted suit with flared trousers or a light gray suit with check lapels or even lapels in silver gray moiré taffeta. Sometimes a brown morning suit with a matching hat or gray close fitting coat with a square bottom that reached down to the knees worn with trousers was acceptable. It was definitely a decade of changes.

The following examples show style characteristics found in the 1970s decade.

1970s Bride: Fitted satin gown; full at bottom; mid length veil; short sleeves.
1970s Groom: White tuxedo with white trousers and accessories.

Many cake toppers were personalized; that is, made to resemble the wedding couple. For example, the bride on the topper could be wearing material from the bride's actual wedding gown. The hair color on the figure could also be changed – in one case (see page 118) the bride figure actually has an interchangeable plastic wig that could be changed to match the bride's hair color. Another type of personalization might be changing the skin tone of the figures. Most of these were personalized by the bride or the baker in the years before the 1950s. Soon after the 1950s, mass produced cake toppers for other ethnic groups became available. The following pictures will show you a few examples of personalization.

This lovely couple is wearing green accented attire for the celebration. I wonder if the real wedding couple was wearing green?

The figures on the left were personalized by having the bride and groom's hair colored red. On the figures in the center, the bride and groom's hair was painted a very dark brown. The figure of the groom on the right was personalized by painting on blond hair and a dark beard.

The bride and groom on the left are placed on a stand with miniature houses and a road leading up to them. I wonder if this signifies "Home Sweet Home." The couple on the right is standing in a grotto made of a shell with other shells surrounding them. One wonders if they lived on the beach or simply loved to visit there.

These are similar styles of figures but all painted differently. The figures on the left have very light skin tone and their eye details appear to be Asian. The figures in the center have red hair and fair skin tone. The figures on the right have very dark hair and a dark skin tone.

The figures on the left have been personalized with the groom wearing a white jacket and the bride wearing a pink fabric gown and hat. The groom on the right wears a black suit and the bride wears a yellow fabric gown. Possibly both of these brides are wearing fabric from the "real" bride's gown.

Both of these figures date to the late 1940s. The figures on the left have been painted by the wedding couple or the baker, since cake toppers weren't being mass produced with dark skin tones during this period. The figures on the right both have painted dark hair.

This is a good example of either a risqué wedding couple or a figure that the bride could dress in the fashion or fabric of her choice. I am inclined to believe the latter is true, but it's more fun to think that the risqué interpretation might be right. In any case, the bride wears lovely underpants and garters attached to her hose. Now that's a blast from the past! She must be from around the 1960s. Some of you reading this may not even know what garters and two pairs of hose were used for. Whatever the case, they make a real cute couple.

Here is an example of an unpainted bride and groom cake topper. It could have been used on a wedding cake as is, but I think I can safely say that it must have been made this way for the bride to paint in the colors of her choice.

The last example is of a topper personalized with separate figures. The bride has a light skin tone and the groom has a dark skin tone. Notice also that the bride is standing on the opposite side.

Determining Values

I have found that the area of the country you live in can make a major difference in the value of cake toppers. In the beginning years of my collecting, from 1989 to 1995, I lived in California. Of course, part of those years included the dawn of the serious cake topper collecting era. During those six years, my collection grew from my first sweet couple to more than three hundred, with very few duplicates. In 1995, we moved to South Carolina. The dealers there virtually seemed unaware that cake toppers existed. Therefore, when I was able to find one, they were reasonably priced. However, my collection was not growing by leaps and bounds as it had in California. Even now, in 2004 and living in Georgia, I don't come across many in the shops. When I do happen upon one, it is not that rare or unusual. Feeling my collecting days were just about over, I then discovered toppers for sale on the Internet. Sources range from on-line collector shops to the very popular on-line auctions. Just because these are available to me, however, hasn't made it any the easier to collect them. The competition is fierce. Prior to the Internet, one of the only real collectors I came in contact with was, surprisingly, a young man who had a fabulous collection. Now I am competing with numerous other collectors and soon-to-be brides. New collectors seem to be joining the fun on a daily basis. Some are anxious bidders who seem to find it necessary to acquire their entire collection within a few weeks. In an on-line auction bidding war, over-

zealous collectors and brides-to-be usually bid the prices up, making it difficult to obtain one of the more desirable pieces at a reasonable price. I am always watching for the lull between these types of bidders, so I can obtain a cake topper for an acceptable price. The interval between such zealous bidders is growing shorter all the time, but I still persevere.

After careful consideration, I have decided not to use the prices established by Internet auctions for this book. The difference in prices from one auction to the next varies greatly, depending on the types and activity of the bidders involved. On one particular day, for example, a cake topper will go for an exorbitant amount and the following week a similar one will be won at a considerably lower price. Therefore, I have established my price ranges from antique shows and markets and they reflect what you would expect to see toppers selling for at antiques malls or shops across the country. These are prices that I, as a collector, might be willing to pay. Keep in mind while viewing the examples that some are not perfect; for purposes of this book, however, I am providing the values as though the items were in perfect condition. Starting with the examples shown, use that as your value baseline. You can decide the quality of the one you have and adjust the value accordingly.

Rarity, age, uniqueness, and quality should be governing factors in determining value. However, there are exceptions. If you are lucky enough to find a very rare, old, or unusual topper with some minor damage, don't pass it by. You may never see it again, especially if it is of the homemade variety or made from a food product. One aspect of rarity is the survival rate of these items. Many have either been broken because of their fragility or tossed away after the wedding or, unfortunately, after a couple splits up. I believe that is why I have found many brides all by themselves. You can expect to find some discoloration, either because of old age or cake residue. That doesn't seem to be a problem with most collectors. Broken off parts or major cracks do affect desirability and value. As noted, I have listed my high and low values based on the pieces being in perfect to near perfect condition – with the exception of some discoloration, which is considered acceptable. If you find a topper with damage, always expect to pay less than the values shown in this book. You can also expect to pay more for toppers made of food products. This applies to food product bases as well, because of the fragility (not to mention their problematic survival rate due to humidity, being eaten by bugs, or other damaging effects). Also, the more elaborate the cake topper, the more valuable it becomes.

I would like to mention quality again here, because I want to stress that quality should be a major factor in your selection. There are collectors who collect only German or only Japanese figurines; however, you can expect to pay slightly more for figurines from Germany because of their superior quality.

The type of wedding cake topper also affects the value. Some collectors look for cake toppers that show the figures wearing occupational attire. The vintage ones are rare, and unfortunately I don't have an example, but I have seen celluloid Kewpie figures that were wearing medical attire. The groom wore a crepe paper suit with "MD" on his hat and the bride wore a white crepe paper nurse's uniform with an apron. The bride's cap and the front of her uniform had a "red cross" emblem on them. Both figures appeared to be of World War I vintage. You can expect to pay more for this type of topper.

Similarly, although I haven't seen one, I have heard that there are vintage cake toppers depicting the wedding couple enjoying a favorite hobby, such as golf, tennis, badminton, horseback riding, etc. Since these figures are rare and very collectible, you would expect to see much higher prices on these types of toppers. There are many occupational as well as hobby oriented bride and groom cake toppers being manufactured today that will one day be very valuable.

There are some cross collectibles that are sought after not only by collectors of cake toppers, but also by a variety of other collectors – these include the Kewpie, music box, and unique lamp collectors. Some people collect "Made in Japan" or "Occupied Japan" marked items. Many such collectors will purchase a wedding cake topper with these marks just for the marks alone. Still another example would be collectors of military memorabilia, who will snap up wedding cake toppers with soldiers on them. The military cake toppers are fabulous, so if you find one, grab it. They are very hard to obtain and very valuable. If you are able to find World War II toppers, you can expect to pay more for them than for military toppers of later decades. And, if you are lucky enough to find one from that era containing a vintage flag, it will be even more valuable. If there are two flags, the value goes up even more. The more flags, the more you can expect to pay. Remember, in any of these cross collectible categories you are dealing with more competition – hence, higher values.

Some collectors specialize in particular eras, but I find that the majority of collectors, like me, collect every time period and every variety available in the market. Whatever style you decide to collect, have fun accumulating the kind of cake topper that suits your tastes, and have fun doing it!

Composition –
What Is Your Topper Made Of?

Listed below are brief descriptions of the various types of materials used to make the cake toppers shown in this book. Note that in categorizing individual toppers shown in Chapter 4, I took into consideration that some were made out of different materials within the figure itself. As these types could fall into more than one of the categories in that chapter, I will list the topper under the composition that the head is made of.

Bisque – Unglazed white porcelain.
Celluloid – A highly flammable substance made from a material composed essentially of gun cotton and camphor. When pure, it resembles ivory in texture and color, but can be colored to imitate coral, tortoise shell, amber, malachite, etc. It is used in the manufacture of jewelry and many small articles, such as combs, brushes, collars, cuffs, and of course cake toppers. Originally called xylonite.
Crepe Paper – Crinkled tissue paper, resembling the fabric crepe, used for decorations.
Earthenware or **Ceramic** – Earthenware is the type of slip used to produce most hobby ceramic items. It is a slightly porous opaque pottery fired at a low heat.
Food By-Products – hereafter described as food product(s)
  Marzipan – A paste made with ground almonds and sugar that can be molded into almost any shape. The composition is then sculpted and painted; the result is an edible decorative item. There are many stories about the origin of marzipan. According to Werner, a Master Baker from Germany, marzipan was created several hundred years ago. There was a great drought in Italy and almonds were the only substantial crop to survive. Consequently, people

learned many new ways to use and eat almonds. They made almond bread, almond pie, almond soap, and almond pastries. During this period, someone created marzipan. It was so well liked that the use of this product was continued. Eventually, it reached Lubeck and Hamburg in Germany, where it is still made today. The recipe they use is based on an old traditional recipe and is considered the finest in the world.

Gum Paste – A candy clay made of confectioners' sugar and other ingredients to create an elasticity to mold and ability to harden when dry. There are many different recipes, but the one probably used most often consists of confectioners' sugar, water, and glucose. Some recipes call for the addition of a coagulant, gum tragacanth (also known as gum trag).

Pastillage – A sugar paste that is basically the same as gum paste, but made without using glucose. It was used to make bells and other decorations.

Spun Sugar – Boiled sugar that is made into long, thin threads by dipping wires into the sugar syrup and weaving them so that the sugar falls off in fine streams.

Glass – A hard, brittle, translucent, and commonly transparent substance, white or colored, made by fusing together sand or silica with lime, potash, soda, or lead oxide.

Marble Composite – This is a name I invented due to the lack of technical information. The figures under this heading appear to be cold to the touch and have a gritty texture. The are also heavy in weight. I suspect these items were molded, since there are mold marks.

Metal – For the purpose of this book, the metal cake toppers described are made from a cast metal or a die-cast process, probably using a lead or zinc alloy. These objects were made with a molten metal and molded into the shape of the final product.

Papier Mâché – A substance made by processing and using a mixture of paper and natural glues.

Parian – During the 1840 era, a new hard, white unglazed porcelain known as "statuary porcelain" and later as "Parian" from its marble-like quality was first produced by Spode. Sculptors produced statuary in scaled-down models of larger pieces.

Pipe Cleaner – A pliant, tufted, narrow rod normally used for cleaning a pipe stem but also used for decorating.

Plaster of Paris or **Chalkware** – Any of several gypsum cements; a white powder (a form of calcium sulphate) that forms a paste when mixed with water and hardens into a solid. Used in making molds and sculptures as well as casts for broken limbs.

Plastic – Plastic is a common name for polymers: materials made of long strings of carbon and other elements. Each unit in a string is called a monomer, and is a chemical usually derived from oil. There are many different types of plastic, depending on the compounds added. Plastic is capable of being molded into many different shapes.

Thermoplastics soften with heat and harden with cooling. Some typical thermoplastics we are familiar with are acrylic, nylon, polythene, PVA, PVC, and Teflon.

Thermosets are cured or hardened by heat. Some typical thermosets we are familiar with are Bakelite, epoxy, melamine, polyester, and polyurethane.

Porcelain – A hard, white, translucent ceramic made by firing a pure clay and then glazing it with various colored fusible materials. Fine china is made of this substance.

Spun Glass – Same as above, but spun into various shapes while very hot.

Manufacturers and Their Products

The following list of manufacturers is by no means all inclusive. Many manufacturers never marked their cake toppers and have long since gone out of business. A number of other early manufacturers are still in business today, starting their early process with food product and progressing with the times to the material of the day. This list was compiled from various cake topper examples shown in this book. The manufacturer or country is listed as marked on the cake topper, i.e., the figures, base, or the original container or box that the topper came in. If I was able to find additional information, I have added it beside the company or country of origin in the list. I am sure there were, and are, many more. Also, I have found that there were thick and heavier plastic pieces used in the late 1930s and early 1940s, as mentioned earlier. I do not know who manufactured them, but some appear to have possibly been cast from the same molds as their earlier bisque counterparts. They do look very much alike.

For convenience, I have listed the manufacturers by category of material composition, and the categories are shown in chronological order as they were used to manufacture cake toppers. The order of their appearance is: food product, porcelain or bisque, celluloid, crepe paper, metal, plaster of Paris (chalkware), ceramic, and plastic. This should help in determining the age of a cake topper as well.

Confectioners of Food Products
(Note: With the exception of those from J. N. & Company, all the other food product cake toppers in this book are not marked. I have noted below some additional companies I discovered while doing my research. The balance of the list was compiled from known confectioners' trade catalogues.)

Cadbury Brothers, Ltd., Worcestershire, England
Earnest Schülbe, Manchester, England
J. N. & Company, Chicago, Illinois
Pfeil & Holing, Inc, Woodside, New York, USA (this is
    questionable)
Schall & Co., New York, New York, USA
Sparagnapane & Co., London, England
Tom Smith & Co., London, England

Bisque

Argent Novelty Ornaments, USA
Empress – Japan
Germany
Hertwig & Co., Germany (1890-1937)
Japan
P&H
Pioneer Merchandise Co., New York (made in Japan)
SHACKMAN

Celluloid

C. A. Reed Co., Williamsport, Pennsylvania, USA
J. N. & Co., Chicago, Illinois, USA
Japan (several different identifying marks)
Pascall
SHIMMIKN

Crepe Paper
Adler Favor and Novelty Co., St. Louis, Missouri

Metal

Barclay, West Hoboken, Union City, and North Bergen,
    New Jersey (1924-1971)

Chalkware

Arco Products, New York
A. Silver
ACA
Adolph Kyer, Germany
Calif. Burnham SC
Coast Novelty Mfg. Co., Venice, California (AKA Coast
    Novelty Co.)
Cypress Novelty Corp., Brooklyn, New York
DelvinSonal Co.
J. Levinsohn, USA
Mane
Marblelike Novelty Co., USA (Marblelike Co. possibly
    Germany also)

Mellillo Studios
P&H (not sure if this is also a mark for Pfeil & Holing)
Pfeil & Holing, Inc, Woodside, New York, USA
Rainbow Doll Co.
Rex Novelty Co.
RMM
Roby Rich
RxM. Co. N. Y.
Wilton Enterprises, Chicago, Illinois, USA

Ceramic and Porcelain

Enesco, Itasca, Illinois, USA (1958 to present)
Inarco
Josef Originals, California, USA (1940s-1985)
Lefton (Leftons)
Made in Japan
Napco Ceramic (Napcoware)
Norcrest (Japan)
Ruben Originals
Vcagco Ceramics Japan

Plastic

Amidan Specialties, Ogden, Utah, USA
Anderson and Assoc., Palos Verdes, CA (Made in Hong
    Kong)
By Bush
Charm Spec. Co., NYC, NY
Coast Novelty Mfg. Co., Venice, California, USA (AKA
    Coast Novelty Co.)
Cypress Novelty Corp., 317 Eaton St., Brooklyn, New
    York, USA
Heartland Plastics Inc.
Japan
Katat, Hong Kong
L. Karp & Sons
Lomey Mfg., Deer Park, New York, USA
Made in Canada
Made in Hong Kong
Made in Hong Kong, "KT" in circle
Parrish's, Los Angeles, California, USA (Hong Kong)
Pfeil & Holing, Inc, Woodside, New York, USA
Vanguttman Co., Cincinnati, Ohio, USA
Wilton Enterprises, Chicago, Illinois, USA (Hong Kong,
    Mexico)
Wilton, Woodridge, Illinois (Hong Kong)

Chapter Four

The Wedding Album

Traditional

Food Product

c. 1890. No marks. Probably American or English made. The figures and base are made of molded food product. Very detailed, especially their faces and hands. Hand painted details. There is a bustle incorporated into her gown and she has tiny lace and satin ribbon detail affixed to her gown. She wears her original tulle veil. Behind them is a single covered wire that is decorated with fabric flower and leaves. It curves up and over their heads, and centered there is a silver bell made of glass. 2.75" each. Overall height 8". Very delicate and rare. *Courtesy of Mary Swafford. Photographed by Kylie Antolini.* $220-260.

c. 1895. No marks. Probably American or English made. The entire topper is made of a molded food product, including the bride, groom, dove, and base (backed with netting). Both the bride and groom stand separately and have intricate body and costume details including their hand painted details. The bride has real lace trim on the bottom of her gown and neck and wears a tulle veil. The figures stand under a wire arch adorned with fabric flowers and a dove. Groom 2.75". Bride 2.5". Overall height 10.5". Came with glass dome. Very delicate and rare. $340-380.

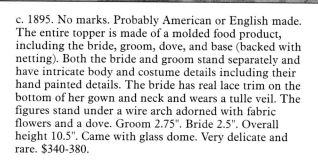

c. 1900. No marks. Probably American or English made. The entire topper is made of a molded food product, including the bride, groom, base, and the bell, which has the words "MARRIAGE" printed in gold letters. Both the bride and groom stand separately and have intricate body and costume details including their hand painted details. The bride has real lace trim on her gown and wears a tulle veil. The base is backed with netting and is decorated with an arch of fabric flowers. Attached to the arch are a mercury glass bell and a silver foil horseshoe decorated with fabric flowers and a paper bow that were probably used as table or cake decoration then added later to the cake topper as part of the memento. Bride 2.25". Groom 2.5". Overall height 9". Came with a glass dome. Very delicate and rare. $340-380.

c. 1900. No marks. Probably American or English made. The entire topper is made of a molded food product, including the bride, groom, bell, dove, base (backed with netting), and horseshoe with the words "GOOD LUCK" in gold letters. Both the bride and groom stand separately and have intricate body and costume details including their hand painted features. Large, decorative wire arch is adorned with fabric flowers. The bell has the word "Marriage" written in gold letters, and inside it is another very thin glass bell. Bride wears a net veil. Notice the bride stands on the opposite side. 3.5" each. Overall height 16". Very delicate and rare. *Courtesy of Mary Swafford. Photographed by Kylie Antolini.* $350-400.

c. 1915. Not marked. Probably American or English made. Bride and groom stand separately and are made from a molded food product and have hand painted details. These figures came with other wedding memorabilia including a gown dated to the 1930s. However, I believe these figures to be earlier. They once stood on a molded food product base. The wire arch is decorated with fabric flowers and has a mercury glass bell attached. The arch has a connecting base made of food product. Bride 2.75". Groom 3". Very delicate and rare. Topper without memorabilia $110-130.

c.1910. Not marked. Probably American or English made. Bride and groom stand separately and are made from a molded food product and have hand painted details. The bride wears a net veil. Bride 3". Groom 3.25". Rare. $100-120.

c. 1915/20. Not marked. Probably American or English made. Bride and groom stand separately and are made from a molded food product and have hand painted details. The figures stand on a food product base with a net backing and under a mercury glass bell attached by a wire stand adorned with fabric flowers. 3" each. Overall height 14". Very delicate and rare. $150-180.

c. 1915. Not marked. Probably American or English made. Bride and groom stand separately and are made from a molded food product and have hand painted details. The figures stand on a food product base backed with netting. The bride wears a full length veil. Bride 2.5". Groom 2.75". Overall height 4.5". Very delicate and rare. $120-150.

c. 1915. Not marked. Probably American or English made. Bride and groom stand separately and are made of a molded food product and have hand painted details. The figures stand on a food product base backed with netting. The groom has long tuxedo tails. The bride has a detailed gown with a draped skirt. Over the shoulders, and around the bodice, fine net lace has been added for detail. This is the same fine netting that is also used on her floor length veil. The figures are attached by metal posts that protrude through the bottom of the base, up into their feet. From the base are wire arches that are covered with fabric flowers. The tall piece in the center back curves over the couple and hanging above their heads is a silver glass bell. 3.5" each. Overall height 13". Very delicate and rare. *Courtesy of Mary Swafford. Photographed by Kylie Antolini.* $195-220.

c. 1930/40. Not marked. These types of figures appear to have been used throughout the 1930 and 1940 era, only in different compositions such as bisque, chalk, and (like this one) molded food product with hand painted detail. The base is also made of molded food product backed with netting and has two wire arches adorned with twisted satin ribbon and fabric flowers, which, I believe, were added at a later date. Two food product bells connect the arches at the top. Figures 4.25". Overall height 8". Very delicate and rare. $80-100.

c. 1920. Not marked. Probably American or English made. Bride and groom stand separately and are made of a molded food product and have hand painted details. They stand on a cookie shaped food product base. The base has been glued to a cylinder shaped piece of cardboard to give it additional height, and then covered with stiff netting. The bride has a flower on each side of her head that holds a delicate net veil. The figures are attached to the base by metal posts that protrude upward and into their feet. There is a wire paper covered arch coming from the base and decorated with fabric flowers. Bride 2.25". Groom 2.5". Overall height 6". Very delicate and rare. *Courtesy of Mary Swafford. Photographed by Kylie Antolini.* $180-210.

c. 1930/40. Not marked. This type of figure appears to have been used throughout the 1930 and 1940 era, only in different compositions such as bisque, chalkware, and (like this one) molded food product with hand painted detail. The base is made of a molded food product and a wire arch is decorated with fabric flowers. Figures 4.25". Overall height 8". Very delicate and rare. $60-80.

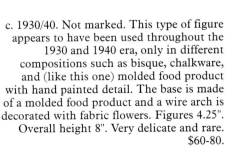

c. 1940. If marked, not visible. Hand painted detail. Figures, vase, and base are made of food product. Behind the figures on the base is a vase or pocket into which the fabric flower sprig is inserted. Figures 3". Overall height 7". Very delicate and rare. *Courtesy of Mary Swafford. Photographed by Kylie Antolini.* $65-75

c. 1940. Not marked. Figure and base are made of molded food product and have hand painted details. Figures 3.5". $25-30.

c. 1920. If marked, not visible. Possibly made in Germany. Hand painted detail. Base and bell made of molded food product and decorated with fabric flowers, and organdy ribbon. Figures 2.25". Overall height 5". $115-135.

c. 1920. Stamped "Germany" in black ink. Hand painted details. A note that came with the figures, in a hankie box, read "Trinket given to bride in 1920." Figures 2.25". $35-45.

c. 1920. Not marked. Possibly Germany. Hand painted details. Figures 2.75". $40-60.

c. 1920. Stamped "Germany" in red ink. Base and figures are one piece. Hand painted details. Figures 4.25" $80-100.

c. 1920. Not marked. Bride and groom stand separately and have hand painted detail. The bride is adorned with tiny silver flowers on her head that are attached to a tulle veil. The figures are standing on a multi level base made of food product. They are attached by a small metal post. Behind the figures is an intricate structure resembling a church door. There are four paper covered wire sprays, with two on each side. Two have fabric lily of the valley sprays with silver paper leaves, and the two longer sprays to the back have fabric and silver leaves. The lower sprays were inserted into the base. The upper sprays were inserted into the molded holders that were made as part of the back side of the church door. Notice that the bride stands on the opposite side. Figures 2.25". Overall height 5.25". Very delicate and rare. *Courtesy of Mary Swafford. Photographed by Kylie Antolini.* $195-220.

c. 1930. Possibly earlier. If marked, not visible. Base that the figures stand on has a paper label reading "ARGENT Novelty Ornaments No. 210, Made in U.S.A." The number "210" is handwritten. Hand painted details. The figures are attached by inserting a cord into the satin covered cardboard base. The large, round decorative arch is covered in the same satin material. It is decorated with fabric flowers and a satin covered cardboard bell. The bride wears a long tulle veil. Figures 3.75". Overall height 9.5". *Courtesy of Mary Swafford. Photographed by Kylie Antolini.* $95-110.

c. 1930. If marked, not visible. Hand painted detail. Base and bell, backed with netting, are made of food product and decorated with fabric flowers and a silk ribbon. On top of the bell is the word "MARRIAGE." Figures 3". Overall height 5". *Courtesy of Mary Swafford. Photographed by Kylie Antolini.* $95-110.

c. 1920/1930. Incised "Germany" on the bottom. Hand painted details. Wedding gown is possibly 1930s style. Hairstyle and headband are 1920s style. Possibly from Hertwig & Co. in Germany. Figures 5.25". $100-125.

c. 1920/1930. Incised "Germany" on the back of base. Bride and groom stand separately and have hand painted details. Wedding gown is possibly 1930s style. Hairstyle and headband are 1920s style. Possibly from Hertwig & Co. in Germany. Bride and groom 6". $160-190.

c. 1920/1930. Stamped "Germany" in black ink on bottom. Incised "Germany" and "4544" on the back of base. Hand painted details. Wedding gown is possibly 1930s style. Hairstyle and headband are 1920s style. Figures 3.75". $60-80.

c. 1920/1930. Separate figures. Bride incised "8065 Germany" and groom is incised "4497". Both have hand painted detail. Bride wears a tulle veil. Wedding gown is possibly 1930s style. Hairstyle and headband are 1920s style. Possibly made by the Hertwig Co. in Germany. Bride just over 7". Groom 7.5". $160-220.

c. 1920/1930. Bride incised "5170/2/0 Germany" and groom incised "5120/2/0". Separate figures. Hand painted details. Wedding gown is possibly 1930s style. Hairstyle and headband are 1920s style. Possibly made by the Hertwig Co. in Germany. Bride 5". Groom 5.25". $150-180.

c. 1930, possibly earlier. Incised "Japan" on groom's back. Hand painted details. Wedding gown is 1930 style. Hairstyle and headband are 1920 style. This appears to be an imitation of German figures. Figures 6.75". $65-80.

c. 1930. Before WWII. Marked "Japan" stamped in black ink. Hand painted details. Figures 7". $50-70.

c. 1930. Before WWII. Incised "Germany". Hand painted details. Figures 2.75". $30-40.

c. 1930. Three piece set all marked "Japan" stamped in red ink. The set includes a bride, groom, and preacher. They have a matt glaze finish and hand painted details. The set comes in their original box that is marked on the bottom "680/126, 3 pieces, Made in Japan". 3" each. $20-35.

c. 1930/40. I believe these were probably used before, then again after WWII, since I have seen vacation souvenirs of these figures dating to the late 1940 period. Bride's attire appears to be in the fashion of the 1930 era. Stamped "Made in Japan" in red ink on the bottom. Hand painted detail. On the front of the base are the words "Our Wedding Day". Figures 4". $25-40.

c. 1930/40. I believe these were probably used before, then again after WWII, since I have seen vacation souvenirs of these figures dating to the late 1940 period. Bride's attire appears to be in the fashion of the 1930 era. The figures are separate. The bride is stamped "Japan" in red ink. No marks on the groom. Hand painted detail. 2.75" each. $25-40.

c. 1930/40. I believe these were probably used before, then again after WWII, since I have seen vacation souvenirs of these figures dating to the late 1940 period. Bride's attire appears to be in the fashion of the 1930 era. Stamped "Japan" in black ink on the bottom. Hand painted detail. On the front of the base are the words "Our Wedding Day". The figures are covered with a glass dome. Figures 3.25". $30-40.

c. 1930/40. I believe these were probably used before, then again after WWII, since I have seen vacation souvenirs of these figures dating to the late 1940 period. Bride's attire appears to be in the fashion of the 1930 era. Hand painted detail. The figures stand separately on a food product base decorated with fabric and silver foil flowers. Figures 3" including base. $50-60.

c. 1930/40. I believe these were probably used before, then again after WWII, since I have seen vacation souvenirs of these figures dating to the late 1940 period. Bride's attire appears to be in the fashion of the 1930 era. No marks are visible, but they are probably marked Japan. Hand painted details. It doesn't appear this cake topper has ever been used since it is still in the original cellophane wrap. The base is cardboard covered with fabric ribbon and has a heart shaped wire arch decorated with fabric flowers, ribbon, and lace. Figures 2.75". Overall height 6.75". $45-55.

c. 1930/40. I believe these were probably used before, then again after WWII, since I have seen vacation souvenirs of these figures dating to the late 1940 period. Bride's attire appears to be in the fashion of the 1930 era. Stamped "Made in Japan" in red ink on the bottom. Hand painted detail. On the front of the base are the words "Our Wedding Day". Figures 4". $25-40.

c. 1930. Stamped "Japan" in black ink on the bottom. Hand painted detail. Figures 4". $25-30.

c. 1930. Black ink smudged on the bottom, probably a "Japan" stamp. Hand painted detail. Figures 4". $25-30.

c. 1930. Incised "Japan" on groom's coat tails. Hand painted detail. Hair on bride and groom painted gold. Figures 3.5". $20-30.

c. 1930. Incised "Japan" on the back of base. Hand painted detail. Figures 4". $25-35.

c. 1930. Both bride and groom have "Japan" incised on their backs and stamped "Japan" on the bottom. The bottom of the box is stamped "Made in Japan". Hand painted detail. The bride wears a long net veil. The box has old paper scrap with the sentiment "Come to me my darling, when're I need a friend. I know that thou art faithful, and will be to the end." 2.75" each. Without box $20-30. With box and note $25-35.

c. 1930. Incised "Japan" on the back of base. Also, faint red stamp "Japan" on the bottom. Hand painted detail. The bride has a fabric flower on her shoulder. Figures 4". $25-35.

c. 1930. Stamped "Japan" in black ink on the bottom. Hand painted detail. Figures 4". $25-35.

c. 1930. Stamped "Japan" in black ink on the bottom. Hand painted detail. Figures 3" $20-30.

c. 1930. If marked, not visible. Probably Japan. Hand painted detail. Food product base embellished with fabric flowers. Bride wears a net veil. Figures 4" including base. $35-50.

c. 1930. Incised "Japan" on the back of groom. Hand painted detail. Base is made of food product backed with netting. It is decorated with fabric flowers and food product cherubs and birds. The birds are holding silver metal rings. There are two wire arches that are held together at the top by two papier mâché bells covered with silver foil. This is topped with satin and organza ribbon. Figures 3.5". Overall height 7.5". $80-90.

c. 1930. Incised "Germany" on the bottom of the bride's gown. Hand painted detail. Figures stand on a food product base backed with netting and a wire arch adorned with fabric flowers and a bisque cupid flying overhead. The bride wears a net veil. Figures 3.75". Overall height 11". $140-160.

c. 1930. Incised "Germany" on the bottom of the bride's gown. Hand painted detail. Food product base backed with netting is stamped with "1499" on the bottom and is decorated with fabric flowers. Bride wears a net veil. Figures 3.5" including base. $75-85.

c. 1930. If marked, not visible. Probably Germany. Figures have hand painted detail and stand on a food product base. Above them is a wire arch adorned with swirls of ribbon, fabric flowers, and two glass bells. Bride wears a net veil. Figures 3". Overall height 6.5". $115-135.

c. 1930. Incised "Germany" on the bottom of the bride's gown. Hand painted detail. Food product base backed with netting and has two wire arches adorned with fabric flowers and a food product bell above the figures. Bride wears a net veil. Note with this topper states that the wedding took place in August 1930. Figures 3". Overall height 7.25". $120-140.

c. 1930. If marked, not visible. Probably Germany. Hand painted detail. Base, pillars, canopy, and birds are all made of molded food product. The bell is bisque. The base is decorated with fabric flowers. Bride wears a net veil. Hand-written note on the bottom of the base reads: "Nellie Thompson married to Judson Atkins, Sept. 4th 1937". Figures 3". Overall height 6". Very delicate. $120-140.

c. 1940/1950. Probably after WWII. Stamped "Japan" in black ink. Hand painted detail. Figures 6.5". $30-40.

Unknown date. Faint red stamp looks like "Germany". They appear to be from the 1920 or the 1930 era. Hand painted details. Figures 3.75". If Germany, $35-45.

c. 1940/1950. Probably after WWII. Stamped "Japan" in red ink. Hand painted detail. Figures 3.75". $15-25.

c. 1940/1950. After WWII. Incised "Occupied Japan" on groom's back. Hand painted detail. Figures 3.25". $20-25.

c. 1940/1950. After WWII. Stamped "Made in Occupied Japan" in black ink. Hand painted detail. Figures 4". $20-25.

c. 1940. No marks. Glazed over bisque. Hand painted detail. Note that came with cake topper states "Married in the 1940s and the bride's husband was lost at sea on a fishing boat". Figures 4.5". $25-35.

c. 1940. The figures on the left are incised "Made in Occupied Japan". The figures on the right are marked "Made in Japan" and molded a little fuller, yet both figures are very similar. Hand painted detail. Both figures measure 4". $25-35.

c. 1940/1950. After WWII. Stamped "Made in Occupied Japan" in red ink. Hand painted detail. 4". $25-35.

c. 1940. If marked, not visible. Hand painted detail. Beach motif. Figures stand on a plaster base decorated with gold glitter sea shells. Possibly one-of-a-kind example. Figures 3.5". Overall height 6". $65-85.

c. 1940. Incised "Japan" on the back of base. Also stamped, in black, the number "10" in a circle. Hand painted detail. Figures 3". $15-20.

c. 1940. Incised "P&H" on the back of base. Hand painted detail. Figures 6.25". $30-40.

c. 1950/1960. Not marked. Hand painted detail. Figures stand on a plastic base with a wire arch decorated with fabric flowers. Figures 4". Overall height 7". $15-25.

c. 1950/1960. Not marked. Hand painted detail. Figures stand on a plastic base decorated with fabric flowers. Figures 3". Overall height 5". $15-25.

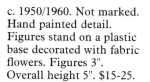

c. 1950/1960. Paper label, "Empress, Made in Japan". Hand painted detail. Figures and base one piece. Base is in the shape of a heart. Similar to chalkware counterparts. Figures 4.25". $20-30.

c. 1960. Incised "1/1" on the bottom. Hand painted detail. Possibly a Lewin Novelty Import Co. example. Figures 4". $15-20.

c. 1960. Not marked. Hand painted detail. Figures 4". $15-20.

c. 1960/1970. Not marked. Hand painted detail. Figures 7". $10-15.

c. 1960/1970. Not marked. Hand painted detail. Figures stand on a plastic base marked "By Bush" and are adorned with a crescent spray of fabric flowers. These figures are usually found in plastic. The bisque examples appear to be rarer to find. Figures 4.75". Overall height 8". $45-55.

c. 1960/1970. Paper label, "Made in Japan". Hand painted detail. Figures 6". $15-25.

c. 1960/1970. Not marked. Hand painted detail. Figures 2.5". $10-15.

c. 1970/1980. Not marked. Hand painted detail. Figures 4.75". $10-15.

c. 1960/1970. Paper label, "Vcagco Ceramics Japan". Hand painted detail. Figures 4". $15-20.

c. 1970/1980. Not marked. Hand painted detail. Figures 6.25". $15-20.

c. 1920/1930. Incised "Japan" on bride's back. Stamped "Made in Japan" in black ink on the bottom. Hand painted detail. The bride's gown looks to be dated to the late teens or early 1920 era. This example may possibly be a later example, which had once been produced in the 1920 or 1930 era. There are green highlights in the bride's gown that make this an unusual and desirable piece. Figures 3.5". $50-70.

c. 1930. Stamped "Made in Japan" in black ink. The bride's back is incised "Japan". Hand painted detail. Figures 3.5". *Courtesy of Mary Swafford. Photographed by Kylie Antolini.* $35-45.

c. 1930. Not marked. The style of the bride's gown looks to be from the 1930 era. However, this example may possibly be a later example, which had once been produced in the 1930 era. Hand painted detail. Figures 3". $20-30.

c. 1940/1950. After WWII. Rabbi stamped "Japan" in black ink on the bottom. Bride and groom not marked. I bought these figures together; however, they may not have originally been a set. Hand painted detail. Set measures 3.5". Set $35-40. Bride and groom without rabbi $20-30.

Left and below:
c. 1940. Not marked. This is undoubtedly one-of-a-kind. Hand painted detail. The figures are almost as detailed as the early molded food product examples, right down to their tiny hands. However, I don't think these were made from a mold. The base and bells are made of chalkware. The wire heart shaped arch is adorned with chenille, fabric sprays, and bisque flowers and leaves. Bride wears a tulle veil and a long porcelain train. Figures 3.25". Overall height 7.5". One-of-a-kind. Very delicate and rare. $140-180.

c. 1950/1960. Stamped "Japan" in black ink on the bottom. Hand painted detail. Figures 3". $15-20.

c. 1950/1960. Stamped "Japan" in black ink. Hand painted detail. Figures 4.75". $15-20.

c. 1950/1960. Stamped "Japan" in black ink. Hand painted detail. These figures have a religious motif since they both carry a bible. Both figures 5". $25-35.

c. 1960. Not marked. Hand painted detail. Figures 4". $15-25.

c. 1960/1970. Not marked. Hand painted detail. This may also have been used for a prom. Figures 6.5". $15-20.

c. 1960/1970. Not marked. Hand painted detail. Figures 7.5". $15-25.

c. 1970/1980. Not marked. Hand painted detail. Figures 4". $10-15.

c. 1940/1950. Not marked. Hand painted detail. Figures 4.5". $20-30.

c. 1940/1950. Not marked. Hand painted detail. Figures stand on a plastic base coated with sugar. The base has a wire arch that is decorated with fabric flowers and satin ribbon. Figures 4.25". Overall height 7". $35-40.

c. 1940/1950. Not marked. Hand painted detail. Figures stand on a plastic base coated with sugar. The base has a spray of fabric flowers behind the figures. Bride wears a net veil. Figures 4.75". $25-35.

c. 1940/1950. Not marked. Hand painted detail. Figures 4.5". $20-30.

c. 1940/1950. Not marked. Hand painted detail. Figures 4.25". $20-30.

c. 1940/1950. Not marked. Hand painted detail. Figures 4.25". $20-30.

c. 1940/1950. If marked, not visible. Hand painted detail. Base and bell are made of chalkware. The base is decorated with fabric flowers and netting. Food product was used for beading. Bride wears a net veil. Figures 3.75". Overall height 7". $55-70.

c. 1940/1950. If marked, not visible. Hand painted detail. Base and bell are made of chalkware. The base is decorated with fabric flowers and netting. Food product was used for beading. Bride wears a net veil. Figures 4". Overall height 6.25". $55-70.

c. 1950. Not marked, but has remains of a foil label on the bottom. Hand painted detail. One piece. Base in the shape of a heart. Figures 4.5". *Courtesy of Mary Swafford. Photographed by Kylie Antolini.* $30-45.

c. 1940/1950. Incised "Holland © Mold" on the bottom. Hand painted detail. Unusual to find both the bride and groom wearing green. May have been custom painted. Figures 6". $35-45.

c. 1950/1960. Paper label, "Lefton's Reg. U.S. Pat. OFF, Exclusive Japan".
Hand painted detail. All pieces are separate. Set includes a bride, groom, and
two flower girls. Bride and groom 5.25". Flower girls 3.5". $55-75.

c. 1950/1960. Marked "E-629/B" on the bottom. Hand
painted detail. Figures 4.5" $15-20.

c. 1950/1960. Not marked. Hand painted detail.
Figures 3.75". $20-30.

c. 1950/1960. Not marked. Hand painted detail. Figures 4.5". $20-30.

c. 1950/1960. Marked "Made in Japan". Hand painted detail. Bride wears a lace and tulle skirt and a tulle veil with a fabric flower headpiece. She carries a fabric flower bouquet. They stand on a plastic base with feet that is decorated with a garland of tulle. Figures 6.5" Overall height 7". $45-55.

Unknown date. Possibly 1950/1960 era. Not marked. Hand painted detail. The origin appears to be European, possibly Spain. These figures were probably used for a Catholic wedding because of the rosary and bible the bride is carrying. The groom may be wearing a uniform. He is also carrying a bible. Figures 5". $35-45.

c. 1950/1960. Not marked. Hand painted detail. The bride's bouquet looks to be made of porcelain, as does the hair on both the bride and groom. Figures 5.5". $35-45.

c. 1950/1960. Stamped "3B3300" in black in on the bottom. No other marks. Hand painted detail. All one piece. Base is in the shape of a heart. Figures 4.5". $25-40.

c. 1950/1960. Paper label, "Made in Japan". Hand painted detail. All one piece. Base is in the shape of a heart. Figures 4.25". $20-30.

c. 1950/1960. Paper label, "Norcrest Japan". Stamped F-895. Hand painted detail. All one piece. Base is in the shape of a heart. Bride wears heavily starched tulle and lace skirt and a tulle veil. Figures 4.25". $25-35.

c. 1960. Stamped "2198" in black ink on the bottom. No other marks. Hand painted detail. Came wrapped in a newspaper dated 1966. Figures 4". $20-30.

c. 1960. Not marked. Hand painted detail. 5". $20-30.

c. 1950/1960. Not marked. Hand painted detail. All one piece. The names of the wedding couple are written in gold on the top of the base: "Libby Bolding, J. L. Cordell". Overall height 5.75". $25-35.

c. 1940. Not marked. Hand painted detail. These figures have a gritty texture. Figures 3.25". $15-20.

c. 1940. If marked, not visible. Hand painted detail. The figures have a gritty texture. Bell and base are made of food product. The bell is decorated with lace and satin ribbon. Figures 3". Overall height 7". $55-75.

c. 1940. Not marked. Hand painted detail. These figures are very heavy and have a gritty texture. Bride wears a net veil. Figures 6.5". $45-60.

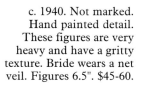

c. 1940. If marked, not visible. Hand painted details. Bride wears a net veil. Base is food product decorated with paper flowers. Minister is bisque and has jointed arms. He is dressed in a crepe paper costume and has painted on glasses. I am sure he was an added piece and did not come with the set. Note with topper reads: "This cake topper was atop of a wedding cake on 11/28/1946. The couple was married until the wife passed away in April 2004. Figures 4". Minister 3.5". Overall height 8.5". $75-100.

c. 1940. If marked, not visible. Hand painted details. Bride wears a net veil. Base made of cardboard with a double wire arch decorated with netting, satin ribbon, and fabric flowers. Figures 3.25" Over height 6.5". $40-60.

c. 1940. If marked, not visible. Hand painted details. Bride wears a net veil. Base made of plastic and decorated with an arch of fabric flowers and paper ribbon. Figures 3.25". Overall height 7.5". $40-60.

c. 1940. If marked, not visible. This may possibly be from the late 1930s era. Hand painted details. Bride wears a net veil. Base is made of food product backed with netting and is decorated with an arch of fabric flowers. Figures 4". Overall height 7". $65-80.

c. 1940. If marked, not visible. This may possibly be from the late 1930s era. Hand painted details. Bride wears a net veil. Base is made of food product backed with netting and is decorated with an arch of fabric flowers. Figures 3.75". Overall height 8.25". $65-85.

c. 1940/1950. If marked not visible. After WWII. These are very similar to figures made by the Marblelike Co. Hand painted detail. Bride's gown has a pearlized finish. The base is made of food product backed with netting, and has a wire arch decorated with fabric flowers. Centered at the top are two chalkware bells that are accented with a satin bow. Figures 5". Overall height 11". *Courtesy of Mary Swafford. Photographed by Kylie Antolini.* $150-165.

c. 1940/1950. Figures marked "copyrighted 1947, Coast Novelty Mfg. Co."
Plastic base marked "Copyrighted 1950, Mfd. By Coast Novelty Mfg. Co.,
Venice, Calif." Bride wears a net veil. Base has two heart shaped arches
decorated with netting. Figures 4.25". Overall height 9". $75-100.

c. 1940. All one piece. Marked "Copyrighted
1949, Bride and Groom Mane". Under the
base marked "Mfg. by Coast Novelty Mfg. Co.,
Venice, California, U.S.A." Hand painted
detail. Base has a wire arch decorated with
fabric flowers and a plastic bell. Figures 3.75".
Overall height 10". $65-80.

c. 1940. If marked, not visible.
Hand painted detail. All one
piece. Bride wears a satin skirt
with a net overskirt, a net veil
with a metallic ribbon headpiece.
She carries a fabric flower and
metallic ribbon bouquet. Notice
the groom's striped gray trousers.
Also, the bride is standing on the
opposite side. The base has a wire
arch decorated with fabric flowers,
paper ribbon, and a chalkware
bell. Figures 9.5". $75-100.

69

c. 1940. Not marked. All one piece. Hand painted detail. Notice that the bride stands on the opposite side. She wears a satin skirt with tulle overskirt and veil, and a silver metallic headpiece. She is carrying a fabric flower and satin ribbon bouquet. Figures 4.25". $40-60.

c. 1940. All one piece. Marked "Copyrighted 1947, Coast Novelty Mfg. Co." on both the outside and underside of base. Hand painted detail. Base has a wire arch decorated with fabric flowers, silver foil leaves, and lace and satin ribbon. Figures 4.25". Overall height 7.5". $60-75.

c. 1940. Both pieces are Marked "Copyrighted 1947, Coast Novelty Mfg. Co." Each is all one piece. Hand painted detail. The figures on the left are painted white and the bride wears a net veil. Figures on the right are painted ivory. Overall height each 5.5". $35-50.

c. 1940. Marked "Copyrighted 1947, Coast Novelty Mfg. Co." Also has a paper label, "Mfg. by Coast Novelty Mfg. Co., Venice, California, U.S.A." All one piece. Hand painted detail. Bride wears a net veil. Base has a wire arch shaped in a heart and decorated with fabric flowers. Figures 4". Overall height 6.75". $55-65.

c. 1940. Marked "Copyrighted 1948, Coast Novelty Mfg. Co., Venice, Calif." All one piece. Hand painted detail. Bride wears a lace skirt and a lace veil. Figures 4". Overall height 5". $35-50.

c. 1940. Not marked. Hand painted detail. Bride wears a net veil. Food product base backed with netting has a double wire arch decorated with fabric flowers and a bell made of food product and backed with netting. Figures 3.25". Overall height 8". $75-85.

c. 1940. Figures marked "A.C.A." Came in plastic container marked "Sweetheart". Hand painted detail. Bride wears a satin and lace skirt and net veil. Base is food product with a net backing and is decorated with a spray of fabric flowers. Figures 4.5". Overall height 9". $60-75.

c. 1940. Marked "Copyrighted, Calif, Burnham SC 1949". All one piece. Hand painted detail. Bride wears a net veil. Notice that the bride is on the opposite side. The base has two arches, one a heart shape, decorated with gathered tulle, satin, fabric and paper flowers, and satin ribbon. Figures 4". Overall height 10.75". $75-95.

c. 1940. Marked "Copyrighted 1948". Hand painted detail. Bride wears a tulle veil. Base is food product with net backing and has a crescent shaped wire arch decorated with fabric flowers. Figures 3.5". Overall height 7.5". $60-80.

c. 1940. Not marked. Hand painted detail. Bride wears a net veil. Base is food product with a net backing and has an arch decorated with fabric flowers and a bell made of food product, backed with lace. Figures 3". Overall height 7". $60-80.

c. 1940. Chalkware base marked with a paper label, "Coast Novelty Mfg. Co., Venice, California, U.S.A." Hand painted detail. Notice the similarity to the bisque figures from the decade before. Wire arch is decorated with organdy, lace, fabric flowers, ribbon, and a chalkware bell. Figures 4.25". Overall height 7.25". $60-80.

c. 1940. Marked "P&H 1949". Hand painted detail. Bride wears a tulle veil. Figures 5.75". $35-55.

c. 1940. All one piece. Marked "P&H 1949". Bride wears a satin skirt with lace and a net veil. The wire arch is decorated with fabric flowers. Figures 6.25". Overall height 7.5". $60-80.

c. 1940. Paper label on bottom, "Mfg. by Coast Novelty Mfg. Co., Venice, California, U.S.A." Hand painted detail. Notice the similarity to the bisque figures from the decade before. Note on bottom: "Top of wedding cake Vida Gardner wed to J.H. (Sonny) Voiers 1/8/48." Figures 7". $60-80.

c. 1940. All examples are made in one piece. All marked "Copyrighted 1947, Coast Novelty Mfg. Co." Figures on left are decorated with a wire arch adorned with lace. Center figures do not have an arch. Figures on right have a wire arch decorated with fabric flowers and came in a box with a note reading "Bride & groom centerpiece of our wedding cake." All figures with base 4". Overall height of toppers with arches 5.5". Each topper has hand painted detail. $30-50 each.

c. 1940. If marked, not visible. Hand painted detail. Base is made of food product with a net backing and has a wire arch decorated with fabric flowers, satin bow, and a plastic bell. Figures 3.75". Overall height 7". $50-60.

c. 1940. If marked, not visible. Hand painted detail. Figures stand on a base made of food product and decorated with a bell made of food product with a net backing. The bell has the word "MARRIAGE" on top and is decorated with netting and fabric flowers. Figures 3.25". Overall height 5.5". $75-100.

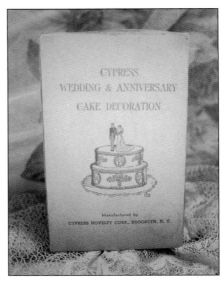

c. 1940. Not marked. Came with original box marked "Cypress Wedding & Anniversary Cake Decoration, Manufactured by Cypress Novelty Corp., Brooklyn, N.Y." Hand painted detail. Bride wears a tulle veil. The chalkware base is made with slots for the cardboard arch, then the arch was decorated with food product flowers. Figures 4". Overall height 4.75". Box measures 3.25 by 5.5". $30-40.

c. 1940. No marks. Probably made by the Cypress Novelty Corp. Hand painted details. Each of these three figures is painted differently. The center figures have a very light skin and Asian shape eyes. They may possibly have been painted for an Asian couple. The figures on the left are from a slightly different mold and have red hair. Figures 3.5" each. $25-30 each.

c. 1940. Not marked. Probably made by the Cypress Novelty Corp. Hand painted detail. Bride wears a net veil. Figures stand on a food product base decorated with paper flowers. Figures 3.75". Overall height 4.25". $30-45.

c. 1940. All one piece. Stamp on bottom is barely readable. It appears to be "1946 —Arco Products, Hand Painted, Made in — N.Y." Hand painted detail. This is similar to the bisque figures from the decade before. Figures 4.25". $30-40.

c. 1940. All one piece. Marked "1947, Melillo Studios U.S.A." Bride wears a pink gown. Figures 5". $35-50.

c. 1940. Marked "Copyrighted 1949, Marblelike Novelty Co." Possibly made in Germany. Hand painted detail. There are holes in the body for flower decoration. Figures 4.25". $25-35.

c. 1940. Not marked. Hand painted detail.
Bride wears a net veil. Figures 3". $15-25.

c. 1940. Marked "P&H". Hand painted detail. Bride wears a net
veil. Base is made of food product and is decorated with a spray of
fabric flowers. Figures 4". Overall height 4.5". $35-50.

c. 1940. Figures marked "A.C.A." Hand painted detail. Base is
chalkware, stamped "891", and decorated with a spray of fabric
flowers. Figures 3.5". Overall height 4.25". $35-50.

c. 1940. Marked "1948 J. Levinsohn
Co. Inc." Hand painted detail.
Figures 4.25". $30-40.

c. 1940. Not marked. Hand painted detail. Bride wears a lace skirt and carries a fabric flower bouquet. Figures 4". $25-35.

c. 1940. Marked "Copyrighted 1948, Rex Novelty Co." Hand painted detail. Unusual to see a personalized African-American couple in the 1940s era. Figures 4". $30-40.

c. 1940. Not marked. All one piece. Hand painted detail. Overall height 6". $40-60.

c. 1940. Marked "Copyrighted 1948 J. Levinsohn Co. Inc." Hand painted detail. Bride wears a tulle veil. Figures 3.25". $20-30.

c. 1940. Not marked. Hand painted detail. Figures 3.5". 20-30.

c. 1940. Not marked. Hand painted detail. Bride wears a net veil. Figures 4". $25-30.

c. 1940. Marked "Copyrighted Coast Novelty Mfg. Co." Also has a paper label on the bottom, "Mfg by Coast Novelty Mfg. Co., Venice, California, U.S.A." Hand painted detail. All one piece. Overall height 4.5". $30-40.

c. 1940 (possibly 1950). If marked, not visible. Hand painted detail. Base made of food product and decorated with fabric flowers. Figures 4". Overall height 4.75". $35-50.

c. 1940. Marked "1947 Melillo Studios U.S.A." Hand painted detail. All one piece. Overall height 4.75". $35-50.

c. 1940. Not marked. All one piece. Hand painted detail. Decorated with two miniature houses, and painted to look like a road is leading to the wedding couple. Unusual. Overall height 6.75". $50-70.

c. 1940. Marked "P&H". Hand painted detail. Base made of food product and decorated with a spray of fabric flowers. Figures 4.5". $35-50.

c. 1940. Marked "Copyrighted 1948 Rex Novelty Co." Hand painted detail. Bride wears a net veil. Figures 4". $30-40.

c. 1940. Marked "Copyrighted 1948, Marblelike Novelty Co." Also, bottom stamped "Made in Germany". Hand painted detail. Figures 5". $60-75.

c. 1940. Not marked. Possibly dates to the 1930 era. Costume dates to an earlier period. Hand painted detail. Figures 4.5". $35-45.

c. 1940. Marked "Copyrighted 1948, J. Levinsohn Co." Hand painted detail. Plastic base (not marked) has a wire arch decorated with fabric flowers, silver foil leaves, satin ribbon, and a plastic bell. Figures 4". Overall height 7.5". $50-65.

c. 1940. Not marked. Hand painted detail. Bride wears a very long lace skirt, tulle veil, and carries a fabric flower bouquet. The base is made of food product and has a net backing. It has a wire arch that is decorated with fabric flowers, satin ribbon, and a plastic bell coated with rock sugar. Figures 4". Overall height 9.25". $80-100.

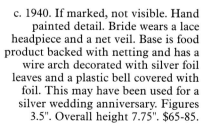

c. 1940. Marked "ACA". Hand painted detail. Similar to bisque counterparts. Figures 3.5". $20-25.

c. 1940. Marked "Copyrighted 1949 Marblelike Co." Possibly made in Germany. Hand painted detail. Bride wears a lace skirt and net veil. Base is food product backed with net and has a double wire arch decorated with fabric flowers. Figures 4.25". Overall height 9". $80-100.

c. 1940. If marked, not visible. Hand painted detail. Bride wears a lace headpiece and a net veil. Base is food product backed with netting and has a wire arch decorated with silver foil leaves and a plastic bell covered with foil. This may have been used for a silver wedding anniversary. Figures 3.5". Overall height 7.75". $65-85.

c. 1940. Incised "Copyrighted 1948. Coast Novelty Mfg. Co., Venice, Calif." Also, stamped under base, " Mfg. by Coast Novelty Mfg. Co, Venice, Calif. U.S.A." Hand painted detail. Bride wears net veil. There is a paper covered wire arch around the figures that is decorated with fabric flowers and leaves. A white plastic bell is centered above them. Figures 5". Overall height 8". *Courtesy of Mary Swafford. Photographed by Kylie Antolini.* $55-65.

c. 1940. If marked, not visible. Hand painted detail. The figures stand on a base made of food product. The dome over the figures is also made of food product and is supported by a paper covered wire arch. The arch goes over the dome. There are cloth leaves and flowers all the way to the top. Centered at the top are a satin bow and a smooth surfaced bell, also made of food product. The base and dome are quite ornate and "lacey". There is stiff netting support under both pieces. Figures 4". Overall height 9.5". *Courtesy of Mary Swafford. Photographed by Kylie Antolini.* $95-125.

c. 1940/1950. Incised "1947" on the back of the bride's gown. The priest has an incised mark "1950 ACA". Hand painted details. Bride, groom, and base are all one piece. Although purchased together, they were not originally sold as a set. The bride and groom measure 5". The priest measures 4.5". *Courtesy of Mary Swafford. Photographed by Kylie Antolini.* $65-70 for set. Couple alone $55-60.

c. 1940. Incised "P&H". Hand painted details. The bride's gown is painted with pearlized ivory paint. She wears her original lace veil. The arch over them is paper covered wire, and decorated with fabric flowers. Figures 4.5". Overall height 7.5". *Courtesy of Mary Swafford. Photographed by Kylie Antolini.* $75-85.

c. 1940. Marked "Copyrighted 1949 Marblelike Novelty Co." Possibly made in Germany. Plastic base not marked. Hand painted detail. Bride wears a satin and lace skirt and a net veil. The base has a heart shaped wire arch with gathered organdy and metallic bric-a-brac. Figures 3.75". Overall height 8". $40-60.

Left:
c. 1940. If marked, not visible. Hand painted detail. The base and dome are made of food product backed with netting and the pillars are made of chalkware. Inside the dome is a thin metal bell. The base is decorated with fabric flowers. Figures 3". Overall height 8.5". *Courtesy of Mary Swafford. Photographed by Kylie Antolini.* $125-145.

c. 1940/1950. Not marked. Hand painted detail. Unusual to find an African-American chalkware couple during this period. Bride wears a net veil. Figures 4.25". *Courtesy of Mary Swafford. Photographed by Kylie Antolini.* $50-55.

c. 1940/1950. Not marked. Hand painted detail. This is a favorite of mine. Very art deco looking. The bride has a Veronica Lake hairstyle from the 1940 era. There is a written notation on the bottom reading "Palm Springs 1952". The base has a wire ribbon arch decorated with ruffled organdy, satin ribbon, and fabric flowers. Figures 4.25". Overall height 8.75". $80-100.

c. 1950. Marked on back, hard to read but looks like "51 J. Levinsohn Co. Inc." Hand painted detail. Bride wears a net veil. Base is made of food product backed with netting and has two wire arches decorated with wrapped paper and fabric flowers, tied together at the top with a chalkware bell and satin ribbon. Figures 3.5". Overall height 9". $45-55.

c. 1950. Four piece set. Bride and groom are marked "ACA". The date is unreadable. The maid of honor is incised "c1957 Pfeil & Holing Inc." Minister incised on back "Copyrighted 1949 Coast Novelty Mfg. Co." and ""Mfg by Coast Novelty Mfg. Venice, California U.S.A. 336" is stamped in black on the bottom. The best man is not marked. All have hand painted details. The bride wears a net veil. At her waist is a bouquet of fabric flowers tied with a satin ribbon. The maid of honor wears a satin blue skirt and a hat of blue fabric flowers. The minister has gray hair and is holding an open prayer book. Bride and groom 4.5". Maid of honor 4.25". Minister 4.25". Best man 4.5". *Courtesy of Mary Swafford. Photographed by Kylie Antolini.* Set $85-95.

c. 1950. If marked, not visible. Hand painted detail. Circular cardboard base is decorated with satin ribbon, a plastic trellis, and fabric flowers. Figures 4". Overall height 7". $40-60.

c. 1950. Marked "Copyrighted 1952 Coast Novelty Mfg. Co."
Plastic base marked "Copyrighted 1950 Coast Novelty Mfg. Co.,
Venice, Calif." Hand painted detail. Decorated with a heart shaped
wire arch, fabric flowers, and a plastic bell. Figures 4.25". Overall
height 10". $40-60.

c. 1950. Marked "1959 J. Levinsohn Co. Inc." Hand painted detail.
Bride wears a long lace skirt and carries a fabric flower bouquet.
She wears a tulle veil. The food product base is backed with
netting and has a wire arch decorated with fabric flowers, satin
ribbon, and a sugar coated plastic bell. Figures 4.25". Overall
height 11". $75-90.

c. 1950. Marked "1958 J.
Levinsohn Co. Inc." Plastic base
not marked. Hand painted
detail. Bride wears a lace skirt,
tulle veil, and a beaded bouquet
and headpiece. Base decorated
with a fabric flowers over wire
arch, strings of pearl beads,
paper bow, and a sugar coated
plastic bell with two beaded
hearts. Figures 4". Overall
height 11.5". $65-80.

c. 1950. Marked "1959 Pfeil & Holing Inc." Hand painted detail. Bride wears a fabric skirt. Figures 4". $25-35.

c. 1950. Marked "Copyrighted 1950, Rainbow Doll Co." Hand painted detail. Bride carries a fabric flower bouquet. Figures 4.5". $30-40.

c. 1950. Marked "Copyrighted 1950 RMM". Hand painted detail. All one piece. Has a wire heart shape decorated with netting and base has a large fabric flower. Figures 3.5". Overall height 7.5". $55-65.

c. 1950. Marked "Copyrighted 1952 Coast Novelty Mfg. Co." Hand painted detail. All one piece. Heart shaped wire decorated with gathered organdy and lace and a large fabric flower. Bride wears a net veil. Figures 4". Overall height 7" $55-65.

c. 1950. Marked "Copyrighted 1952 Coast Novelty Mfg. Co." Plastic base marked "Copyrighted 1959 Coast Novelty Mfg. Co, Venice, Calif., U.S.A." Hand painted detail. Bride wears a long lace skirt and tulle veil. Base has a large wire arch decorated with fabric flowers, satin ribbon, and a glittered plastic bell. Figures 4.25". Overall height 9". $40-60.

c. 1950. If marked, not visible. Hand painted detail. Bride wears a lace skirt. Base is food product and has a wire arch decorated with fabric flowers, satin ribbon, and a chalkware bell. Figures 4". Overall height 9". $55-65.

c. 1950. Marked "Copyrighted 1950 RMM". Hand painted detail. All one piece. Overall height 4.5". $40-50.

c. 1950. Marked "1951 P&H". Hand painted detail. Figures 4.25". $25-35.

c. 1950. If marked, not visible. Hand painted detail. Base is made from a cardboard cylinder decorated with fabric flowers and satin. It has a wire in the back that is decorated with satin ribbon and extends over the figures and ends with a plastic bell. Figures 4". Overall height 7.75". $40-60.

c. 1950. If marked, not visible. Hand painted detail. Bride wears a lace skirt with a net veil and has a fabric flower and paper ribbon bouquet. Food product base is backed with netting and has a wire arch decorated with fabric flowers, paper ribbon, and a plastic bell. Figures 4". Overall height 9.5". $75-100.

c. 1950. Marked "1950 J. Levinsohn Co. Inc." Hand painted detail. Figures have a hole in the center to add flower decoration. Figures 4.25". $25-35.

c. 1950. Marked "1959 Pfeil & Holing". Hand painted detail. Figures 4.25". $25-35.

c. 1950. Marked "Copyrighted 1952 Coast Novelty Mfg. Co." Hand painted detail. All one piece. Bride wears a net veil. Base has a wire arch decorated with fabric flowers and a plastic bell. Figures 5.25". Overall height 8". $55-70.

c. 1950. Marked "1959 Pfeil & Holing". Hand painted detail. Notice that the groom has a painted on beard. Figures 4.25". $25-35.

c. 1950. Marked "1956 Pfeil & Holing". Hand painted detail. Bride wears a full lace and beaded skirt and carries a beaded bouquet. She has her original tulle veil with a rhinestone headpiece. Figures 4.25". $30-40.

c. 1950. Marked "Copyrighted RMM". Hand painted detail. All one piece. Base has two heart shaped wire arches decorated with fluffy netting. Figures 3.25". Overall height 9.5". $ 65-80.

c. 1950. Marked "1951 J. Levinsohn". Hand painted detail. All one piece. Bride wears a net veil. Overall height 6.25" $40-60.

c. 1950. Marked "1959 Pfeil & Holing". Hand painted detail. Base made of food product and has a wire arch decorated with fabric flowers, satin ribbon, and a sugar coated bell. Figures 4". Overall height 6". $40-55.

c. 1950. Marked "Copyrighted 1950 RMM". Hand painted detail. All one piece. Base has a wire arch decorated with fabric flowers, paper ribbon, and a glittered plastic bell. Figures 4". Overall height 7.5". $55-65.

c. 1950. Marked "1959 Pfeil & Holing". Hand painted detail. Bride wears a lace skirt and a net veil. Food product base is backed with netting and has a wire arch decorated with fabric flowers. Figures 4.25". Overall height 8.75". $55-65.

c. 1950. "1956 Pfeil & Holing". Hand painted detail. Base is food product backed with netting and has a double wire arch decorated with fabric flowers, satin ribbon, and a food product bell backed with netting. Figures 4.5". Overall height 11". $75-95.

c. 1950. Marked "1959 Pfeil & Holing". Hand painted detail. Base made of food product and has a wire arch decorated with fabric flowers, satin ribbon, and a plastic bell. Figures 4.25". Overall height 7". $40-55.

c. 1950. Marked J. Levinsohn Inc." Date is unreadable. No marks on plastic base. Base has a wire arch decorated with fabric flowers, satin ribbon, and a silver metal bell. Figures 3.75". Overall height 8". $45-55.

c. 1950. Marked "1959 Pfeil & Holing". Hand painted detail. Two piece base is made of food product and decorated with fabric flowers. Figures 4.25". Overall height 4.75". $40-50.

c. 1950. Figures are marked but unreadable. Hand painted detail. Bride wears a tulle veil. The entire unit, including the base, dome, and pillars, is made of food product. The base is backed with netting and decorated with fabric flowers. Rare to find due to fragility. Figures 3.5". Overall height 10". $100-125.

c. 1950. Marked "1959 Pfeil & Holing Inc." Hand painted detail. Bride wears a long lace skirt. Base is made of food product backed with netting and has a wire arch decorated with fabric flowers and satin ribbon. Handwritten date on bottom reads "June 8, 1958". Figures 3.75". Overall height 7.5". $60-75.

c. 1950. If marked, not visible. Hand painted detail. Bride wears a long lace skirt and a net veil with a beaded headpiece. She carries a beaded bouquet. The plastic base is decorated with a chalk pillar and a circle of gathered netting, plastic beads, fabric flowers, and a sugar coated plastic bell with beads. Figures 4". Overall height 11.5". $65-85.

c. 1950. Marked "Copyrighted 1950 Coast Novelty Mfg. Co." Plastic base marked "Copyrighted 1959, mfd. By Coast Novelty Mfg. Co., Venice, Calif." Hand painted detail. Bride wears a satin skirt and a net veil. Base is decorated with gathered tulle. Figures 4". Overall height 6". $45-55.

c. 1950. Marked "Copyright 1951, Rainbow Doll Co." Plastic base marked "Charm Spec. Co., N.Y.C.N.Y." Hand painted detail. Bride wears a net veil. Base has a wire arch decorated with gathered netting, fabric flowers, a large and small satin bow, and a plastic bell. Figures 4.25". Overall height 9". $65-85.

c. 1950. Marked "A.C.A. 1950". Hand painted detail. Bride wears a net veil. Figures 3.75". $25-35.

c. 1950. Three piece set. Not marked. Hand painted detail. Bride wears a lace skirt and net veil. Set contains the bride, groom, and rabbi. This is how I purchased them, but I am not sure they went together originally. 4" each. $45-55 for the set. Without rabbi $25-35.

c. 1950. Four piece set. Bride and groom marked "Pfeil & Holing Inc. 1957". Minister marked "1950 ACA". Ring bearer not marked. Hand painted detail. Bride wears a yellow satin skirt. Bride, groom, and minister 4.25". Ring bearer 3.25". Set $45-55. Bride and groom alone $25-35.

c. 1950. Not marked. Hand painted detail. The bottom halves of the bride and groom have been cut off, and glued to a wedding cake shaped plastic base which is in turn glued to the bottom of a Fonda half pint cardboard container (as stated on the bottom). From the waist down, there are several layers of lace that cover the entire base. Bride has her original net veil. Overall height 7". *Courtesy of Mary Swafford. Photographed by Kylie Antolini.* $40-50.

c. 1960. Marked "J. Levinsohn Inc. 1962". Hand painted detail. Bride wears a long lace skirt, net veil with a beaded headpiece, and a bouquet of beads. Figures 4". $30-40.

c. 1960. If marked, not visible. Hand painted detail. Bride wears a tulle skirt and veil with a bric-a-brac headpiece and carries a bouquet of fabric flowers and satin ribbon. There are two bases. The bottom base is plastic and topped with a piece of Styrofoam that is covered with satin. There are two double wire arches decorated with tulle, satin ribbon, and fabric flowers. This topper belongs to our very good friends, Eula and Bill McIntosh, who were married on September 30, 1967. See page 10 for a photo of them cutting their wedding cake decorated with this topper. Chalkware figures are harder to find for the 1960 period, as most 1960 figures are made of plastic. Figures 4.5". Overall height 10.5". *Courtesy of Bill and Eula McIntosh.* $40-50.

c. 1940. Not marked. Base stamped "Pat 14484". Hand painted detail. Similar to bisque figures from an earlier decade; this is a plastic version. The bride wears a 1930s style gown and a net veil. Behind the figures are three plastic bells and a dove sitting on top. These are decorated with fabric flowers and silver foil leaves. The base is hard plastic and the back has two plastic horseshoes with the words "Good Luck" on both. Figures 4". Overall height 9". $40-60.

c. 1940. Not marked. Hand painted detail. Similar to bisque figures from an earlier decade; this is a plastic version. The bride wears a 1930s style gown. The figures stand on a plastic base with a wire arch decorated with fabric flowers and silver foil flowers. Figures 3.5". Overall height 8". $30-40.

c. 1940. Not marked. Hand painted detail. Similar to bisque figures from an earlier decade; this is a plastic version. The bride wears a 1930s style gown and a net veil and has long hair. The figures stand on a plastic base with a wire arch decorated with fabric flowers. Figures 3.5". Overall height 6.5". $30-40.

c. 1940. Not marked. Hand painted detail. Bride wears a net veil. The plastic base is decorated with two plastic swans, two plastic bells, a "Good Luck" horseshoe on the back, paper bow, and plastic flowers. It is made to look like the swans are being led by satin reins. Figures 2.5". Overall height 7". $35-45.

c. 1940/1950. Not marked. Hand painted detail. Plastic base has a wire arch decorated with fabric flowers and satin ribbon. Figures 4". Overall height 7.5". $30-40.

c. 1940/1950. Not marked. Hand painted details. Set came together as a bride and groom on a base and the best man and maid of honor connected, without a base. Figures 4" each. Set $25-30.

c. 1940/1950. Not marked. Hand painted detail. Bride wears a beaded satin gown and a fabric flower bouquet. Plastic base has a wire arch decorated with swags of fabric flowers and synthetic beads. Bride and groom are separate. Groom 4.25". Bride 4". Overall height 10.5". $30-45.

c. 1950/1960. Base marked "Pedestal made in Hong Kong, 1959 Copyrighted by Coast Novelty Mfg. Co., Venice, Ca." Hand painted detail. Bride wears a net veil. Plastic base has a wire arch decorated with fabric flowers. Figures 3.5". Overall height 7". $15-20.

c. 1950/1960. Plastic base marked "Copyrighted 1959, Mfg. by Coast Novelty Mfg. Co., Venice, Calif. U.S.A." Hand painted detail. Bride wears a satin skirt and tulle veil with a beaded crown. She carries a beaded bouquet. The base is decorated with a posy of fabric flowers. Figures 4.25". Overall height 9". $25-35.

c. 1950/1960. Figures marked "Copyrighted 1959 by Coast Novelty Co." Plastic base marked "Pedestal made in Hong Kong, 1959 copyrighted by Coast Novelty Mfg. Co., Venice, Calif." Hand painted detail. Bride wears a satin skirt and a gathered tulle veil. Base has a wire arch decorated with fabric flowers and a satin bow. Figures 4". Overall height 7". $20-30.

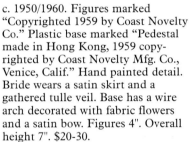

c. 1950/1960. Figures marked "Copyrighted 1959 by Coast Novelty Co." Plastic base marked "Pedestal made in Hong Kong, 1959 copyrighted by Coast Novelty Mfg. Co., Venice, Calif." Hand painted detail. Bride wears a satin skirt and gathered tulle veil. Base has a wire arch decorated with fabric flowers and a satin bow. Figures 4". Overall height 8". $20-30.

c. 1950/1960. Figures marked "Copyrighted 1959 by Coast Novelty Co." Plastic base marked "Pedestal made in Hong Kong, 1959 copyrighted by Coast Novelty Mfg. Co., Venice, Calif." Hand painted detail. Bride wears a satin skirt and gathered tulle veil with a beaded crown. She carries a beaded bouquet. Base has a wire arch decorated with two spun cotton doves with real feathers, fabric flowers, satin ribbon, and a sugar coated plastic bell. Figures 4". Overall height 9.5". $25-35.

c. 1950/1960. Figures marked "Copyrighted 1959 by Coast Novelty Co." Plastic base marked "Pedestal made in Hong Kong, 1959 copyrighted by Coast Novelty Mfg. Co., Venice, Calif." Hand painted detail. Bride wears a satin skirt and gathered tulle veil. Base has a wire arch decorated with fabric flowers and satin ribbon. Figures 4". Overall height 9". $25-35.

c. 1950/1960. Plastic base marked "Copyrighted 1959, Mfg. by Coast Novelty Mfg. Co., Venice, Calif. U.S.A." Hand painted detail. Bride wears a lace skirt and tulle veil with a beaded crown. She carries a beaded bouquet. Base has a large plastic heart with a center lace insert. Figures 4". Overall height 9". $25-35.

c. 1950/1960. Marked "Copyrighted 1959 by Coast Novelty Co." Plastic base marked "Pedestal made in Hong Kong, 1959 Copyrighted by Coast Novelty Mfg. Co., Venice, Calif." Hand painted detail. Bride wears a floor length satin veil. Base has a wire arch decorated with fabric flowers and satin ribbon. Figures 4". Overall height 5.5". $20-30.

c. 1950/1960. Marked "Copyrighted 1959 by Coast Novelty Mfg. Co." Plastic base marked "Hong Kong". Hand painted detail. Bride wears a lace skirt with a tulle veil and beaded crown. Base has a wire arch that is decorated with fabric flowers, satin ribbon, and a plastic bell. Figures 4". Overall height 7.25". $20-30.

c. 1950/1960. Not marked. Hand painted details. Bride wears a lace skirt and tulle veil with a beaded crown. The plastic base is decorated with a posy of blue fabric flowers. Figures 4". Overall height 6.5". $20-30.

c. 1950/1960. Plastic base marked "Vangutman Co., Cincinnati, OHIO, U.S.A." Hand painted details. Bride wears a satin and tulle skirt with a tulle veil and a beaded crown, and carries a bouquet of fabric flowers. The base has a wire arch and is decorated with layers of tulle, fabric flowers, satin ribbon, and a plastic bell. A clear plastic lattice stands behind the figures. Figures 3.75". Overall height 10.5". $30-40.

c. 1950/1960. Plastic base marked "Made in Hong Kong". Hand painted details but no facial painting. A plastic shell stands on the base behind the figures. Notice that the style of the bride's gown dates to the 1930s era. Figures 2.25". Overall height 3.5". $10-15.

c. 1950/1960. Bottom of bride marked "Made in Hong Kong". Hand painted detail. Bride and groom separate. Bride 4". Groom 4.25". $10-15.

c. 1950/1960. Not marked. Hand painted detail. Three piece set of bride, groom, and best man. I'm not sure which one is supposed to be the groom. Bride is dressed in blue. All measure 3.25". Set $10-15.

c. 1950/1960. Base marked "Made in Canada". Hand painted detail. Bride wears a fabric gown with a fabric flower and a net veil with a silver crown that is painted with red dots (to symbolize gems). Figures 3.5". Overall height 5.75". $25-35.

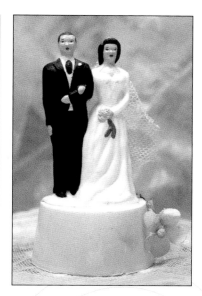

c. 1950/1960. Plastic base marked "214". Hand painted detail. Bride wears a net veil. The base is decorated with a single fabric flower. Figures 3.75". Overall height 4". $10-15.

c. 1950/1960. Not marked. Hand painted detail. Bride is wearing a bright pink satin skirt and a painted, bright pink bodice. Her hat matches her satin skirt and she carries a fabric flower bouquet. The figures stand separately. Groom 4". Bride 3.75". $10-15.

c. 1950/1960. Both figures are separate and are marked "Heartland Plastics Inc." Hand painted detail. The bride doesn't wear a skirt, just her undergarments, garters, and hose. This was probably made for the purpose of personalizing. Unusual. Bride 4.25". Groom 4.5". $20-30.

c. 1950/1960. Both sets of figures are marked "Made in Hong Kong". Hand painted detail. The bride on the left wears a gathered net veil and both she and her groom have dark hair. The bride and groom on the right have red hair. Both 3.75" each. $10-15 each.

c. 1960. Marked "Copyrighted 1963 by Coast Novelty Mfg. Co." Hand painted detail. Bride wears a tulle veil with a beaded crown and carries a beaded bouquet. Figures 4". $10-15.

c. 1950/1960. Bride marked "Made in Hong Kong". Original box marked "Cypress Novelty Corp., 317 Elton St., Brooklyn, New York, 11203." Hand painted detail. Bride wears a lace skirt. Plastic base has a wire arch and is decorated with fabric flowers, satin ribbon, and a plastic bell. Figures 4". Overall height 9". $20-30.

c. 1960. Not marked. Hand painted detail. Plastic base is decorated with a spray of lacy net. Figures 3.5". $10-15.

c. 1960. Base of figures marked "Copyright 1960, Coast Novelty Mfg. Co." Hand painted details. Bride wears a net veil with a single bead headpiece. The plastic base has a plastic arbor and is decorated with netting, fabric flowers, and sugar coated plastic bell. Figures 2.5". Overall height 6.5". $20-30.

c. 1960. Base of figures marked "Copyright 1960, Coast Novelty Mfg. Co." Plastic base marked "Pedestal made in Hong Kong, 1963, copyrighted by Coast Novelty Mfg. Co., Venice, Calif." Hand painted detail. The base has a wire arch that is decorated with fabric flowers, white beads, and a glittered plastic bell. Figures 2.5" Overall height 7.5". $15-25.

c. 1960. Plastic base marked "Katat, Hong Kong". Horseshoe marked "Hong Kong KaT492". Hand painted detail. The large horseshoe with the words "Good Luck" stands on the base and behind the figures. Figures 2.75". Overall height 4.25". $10-15.

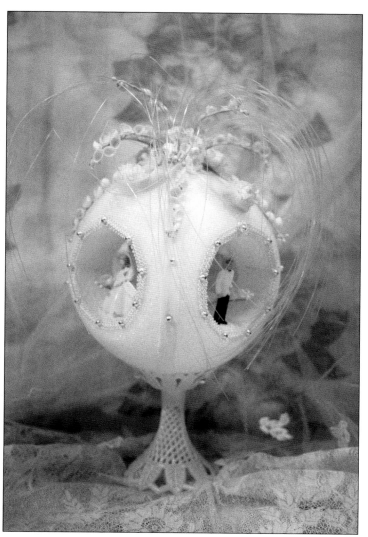

c. 1960. Not marked. Hand painted detail. Two small plastic bride and groom sets decorate this example. They all stand separately in different windows cut from a Styrofoam ball. The ball is decorated with lace bric-a-brac, fabric flowers, velvet ribbon, plastic wire sprays, and pearl beads. It stands on top of a plastic pillar. Figures 2" each. Overall height 12". $20-30.

c. 1960/1970. Bride marked "Wilton Chicago 43, Made in Hong Kong, W.81". Hand painted detail. Bride wears an organdy skirt and veil and carries a bible in her hand. Figures 4.5". $10-15.

c. 1960/1970. Plastic base marked "Made in Hong Kong". Hand painted detail. Bride wears a lace skirt. The figures stand on a two tier base decorated with two silver glittered, plastic angels, three small glittered bells, tulle, and fabric flowers. A plastic, gothic window is placed behind the figures. Figures 3.75". Overall height 11". $30-40.

c. 1960/1970. Marked "Wilton Chicago 43, Made in Hong Kong, W.82". Plastic base marked "Wilton Chicago, 60643, No. 274, Made in Mexico". Hand painted detail. Bride wears an organdy skirt and veil and carries a bible in her hand. The base is decorated with two intertwined plastic wedding bands topped by two plastic doves. Figures 3.25". Overall height 7". $15-20.

...the latest releases and

thousands of books in print,

fill out the back of this card

and return it today!

SCHIFFER PUBLISHING LTD
4880 LOWER VALLEY ROAD
ATGLEN, PA 19310-9717 USA

WE HOPE THAT YOU ENJOY THIS BOOK...and that it will assist at

library. We would like to keep you informed about other publications from Schiffer Books.
Please return this card with your requests and comments. **(Please print clearly in ink.)**
Note: We don't share our mailing list with anyone.

Title of Book Purchased _____

☐ Purchased at: _____ ☐ received as a gift

Comments or ideas for books you would like to see us publish: _____

Your Name: _____

Address _____

City _____ State _____ Zip _____ Country _____

E-mail Address _____

Please provide your email address to receive announcements of new releases

☐ Please send me a **free** *Schiffer Antiques, Collectibles, & the Arts*
☐ Please send me a **free** *Schiffer Woodcarving, Woodworking, and Crafts Catalog*
☐ Please send me a **free** *Schiffer Military, Aviation, and Automotive History Catalog*
☐ Please send me a **free** *Schiffer Lifestyle, Design, and Body, Mind, & Spirit Catalog*

See our most current books on the web at **www.schifferbooks.com**
Contact us at: Phone: 610-593-1777; Fax: 610-593-2002; or E-mail: info@schifferbooks.com
SCHIFFER BOOKS ARE CURRENTLY AVAILABLE FROM YOUR BOOKSELLER

Printed in China

c. 1960/1970. Bride marked "Wilton Chicago 43, Made in Hong Kong, W.82". Plastic base marked "Wilton Chicago, 60643, Made in Mexico". Hand painted detail. Bride wears an organdy skirt and veil and carries a bible in her hand. Base decorated with six curved wire pillars with gathered tulle on top. Figures 3.75". Overall height 6". $10-20.

c. 1960/1970. Bride marked "Wilton Chicago 43, Made in Hong Kong, W.81". Plastic base marked "Wilton Chicago, 60643, W733, Made in Hong Kong". Hand painted detail. Bride wears an organdy skirt and veil and carries a bible in her hand. A single fabric flower posy decorates the base. Figures 4.5". Overall height 5.25". $10-20.

c. 1960/1970. Marks on bride obscured. Plastic base marked "Wilton Woodridge, IL 60517, Hong Kong". Hand painted detail. Bride wears an organdy gown and veil and carries a bible in her hand. The base has a large plastic heart arch and a large plastic glittered bell behind the figures. It is decorated with fabric flowers and tulle. Figures 3.5". Overall height 9". $25-35.

c. 1970. Groom marked "KT (in circle) 1973 Hong Kong". Hand painted detail. Bride wears a lace skirt and a tulle veil. Figures 3". $5-10.

c. 1970. Plastic base marked "Made in Hong Kong, KT (in a circle) No. 559". Hand painted detail. The bride wears a lace skirt and a net veil. The base has a wire arch decorated with fabric flowers, paper ribbon, satin ribbon, and gathered lace. There is another arch behind the forward arch that is made of plastic and in the shape of a heart. Figures 4.25". Overall height 10". $25-35.

c. 1970. Groom marked "Hong Kong No. 1721B". Hand painted detail. Bride wears a lace skirt, net veil, and a beaded crown. Plastic base is decorated with a crescent spray of fabric flowers. Figures 3.25". Overall height 7". $15-25.

c. 1970. Not marked. Hand painted detail. Figures 2". $2-5.

c. 1970. Bride marked "Copyright 1977, Anderson and Assoc., Palos Verdes, Ca. 90274, No. 4948, Made in Hong Kong". Hand painted detail. Notice the groom's sideburns, high heel shoes, and bright blue suit. Bride wears a tulle veil and a beaded crown. Figures 4.75". $10-15.

c. 1970. Plastic base marked "1973 Amidan Specialties, Ogden, Utah". Hand painted detail. Bride wears an organdy veil and carries a fabric flower bouquet. The base has a plastic, heart shaped arch decorated with fabric flowers. Notice the groom's sideburns. Figures 5". Overall height 10". $20-30.

c. 1970. If marked, not visible. Clear plastic base is marked but unreadable. Hand painted detail. Bride wears a lace skirt and beaded crown. This base has two clear plastic arches in the shape of swans standing behind the figures and is decorated with fabric flowers, and satin ribbon. Notice the trendy 1970 era hairstyles on the bride and groom. Figures 4.5". Overall height 8.5". $25-35.

c. 1970. Plastic base marked "1973 Wilton Chicago 60643, 201-205, Made in Hong Kong". Hand painted detail. This example was personalized. Notice that the bride stands on the opposite side. The base has a wire arch and is decorated with fabric flowers and a plastic bell. Figures 3.75". Overall height 11". $25-35.

c. 1970. If marked, not visible. Clear plastic base is marked but unreadable. Hand painted detail. Bride wears a lace skirt and beaded crown. The base is decorated with a large paper fan, fabric flowers, and lace. Notice again the trendy 1970 era hairstyles on the bride and groom. Figures 4.5". Overall height 7". $25-35.

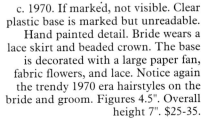

c. 1970. Figures marked "KT (in circle) No. 1970 Made in Hong Kong". Hand painted detail. Bride wears a lace dress and tulle veil. Figures 4.25". $10-15.

c. 1970. If marked, not visible. Hand painted detail. The plastic heart that stands behind the figures is decorated with lace, tulle, satin ribbon, and fabric flowers. The bride wears a lace skirt, tulle veil, and a beaded crown. Figures 4.5". Overall height 8.5". $25-35.

c. 1970. If figures marked, not visible. Plastic base marked "1973 Amidan Specialties, Ogden Utah". Hand painted detail. The bride wears a yellow gown with an organdy veil and carries a single fabric flower. The base and plastic lattice are decorated with fabric flowers, satin ribbon, and angel hair. Notice the sideburns on the groom. Figures 4.5". Overall height 9.5". $25-35.

Unknown date. Possibly
c.1970, but may be as late as
1980. Marked "Parrish's Los
Angeles, Made in Hong
Kong." Figures 4.5". $10-15.

Unknown date. Possibly
dates to c. 1970. Not
marked and unpainted.
These were made to
personalize with one's
choice of color and fabric.
Figures 4.5". $5-10.

c. 1970. Marked "KT (in circle) No. 1970 made in Hong Kong".
Plastic base not marked. Hand painted detail. Bride wears a lace
skirt and tulle veil with a beaded crown. The base and plastic
lattice are decorated with fabric flowers, satin ribbon, and tulle.
Figures 4.25". Overall height 10". $25-35.

c. 1970. Marked "Copyrighted 1974, Coast Novelty Mfg. Co." The plastic base is marked Copyright '59, Coast Novelty Mfg. Co., Venice, CA, U.S.A." Hand painted detail. The bride wears a satin skirt, tulle veil, and beaded crown. The figures stand under a plastic arbor decorated with fabric flowers, tulle, and a sugar coated plastic bell. Notice the date on the base, indicating that the manufacturer was using old stock or an old mold. Figures 4.5". Overall height 9". $25-35.

Left:
c. 1970. Figures marked "Copyrighted 1974, Coast Novelty Mfg. Co." The plastic base is marked Copyright '59, Coast Novelty Mfg. Co., Venice, CA, U.S.A." Hand painted detail. The bride wears a satin skirt and tulle veil with a beaded crown. The base and plastic crescent moon are decorated with lace, fabric flowers, plastic beads, and two glittered bells. These figures were used into the 1980s era. Notice the date on the base, indicating that the manufacturer was using old stock or an old mold. Figures 4.5". Overall height 10". $25-35.

c. 1970. Marked "Copyrighted 1974, Coast Novelty Mfg. Co." The plastic base is marked Copyright '59, Coast Novelty Mfg. Cal., Venice, CA, U.S.A." Hand painted detail. The bride wears a satin skirt, tulle veil, and beaded crown. The base has a wire heart arch decorated with fabric flowers and beads. Figures 4.5". Overall height 8.5". $25-350.

c. 1970. Mark, on wig, "Copyrighted 1971 by — " The plastic base has a wire arch over the figures and is covered with decorative paper and fabric flowers. This appears to be a rare example because of the short gown and the removable rubber hair (wig) on the bride. This particular bride is wearing an auburn wig made of rubber. The wig allowed the baker or cake decorator to change the hair color to match the bride's own hair. Molded into the rubber wig on the back is the copyright information; unfortunately the manufacturer's name is covered by glue. Figures 4". Overall height 7". *Courtesy of Mary Swafford. Photographed by Kylie Antolini.* $45-65.

c. 1970/1980. Not marked. Hand painted detail. Bride wears a fabric gown and tulle veil. Figures 4.75". $10-15.

c. 1940. Not marked. One piece. Hand painted detail. Overall height 4.5". $25-35.

c. 1940. Three piece set. All marked "Barclay, Made in U.S.A." and numbers "620, 625 & 626". Hand painted detail. These were probably made for a child's toy, but may have been used on a wedding cake. 3" each. Set $30.

Chalkware

c. 1940. Not marked. Bride and groom are separate figures. Hand painted detail. The bride wears a floor length net veil. The base is made of food product backed with netting and has a wire arch decorated with fabric flowers and a silk American flag with 48 stars. Bride 3". Groom 3.25". Overall height 7.5". $140-160.

c. 1940. Not marked. Hand painted detail. The bride wears a long net veil. Figures 6.5". $70-90.

c. 1940. Not marked. Hand painted detail. Figures 3.25". $40-55.

c. 1940. If marked, not visible. Hand painted detail. Bride wears a long lace veil. The base is made of food product and has a spray of flowers decorating each side, as well as two paper American flags with 48 stars. Overall height 4.5". *Courtesy of Mary Swafford. Photographed by Kylie Antolini.* $130-145.

c. 1940. Not marked. Hand painted detail. The bride wears a net veil. Base is made of a molded food product and decorated with fabric flowers and a silk American flag with 48 stars. Figures 3.5". Overall height 4.25". $120-135.

c. 1940. Not marked. Hand painted detail. Figures 3.25". $40-50.

c. 1940. Not marked. Hand painted detail. Bride carries a bouquet made of icing and a paper ribbon. Figures 4.25". $50-60.

c. 1950. I am unable to read the maker's mark but it is incised "1950". There is a pencil written mark on the bottom reading "562 Mil". Hand painted detail. The base is chalkware and has a wire arch of fabric flowers plus a paper flag with 48 stars. Figures 4.25". Overall height 7.5". $110-130.

c. 1950. Incised "RxM. Co N.Y." on bride's back. Plastic base is unmarked. Hand painted detail. The bride is wearing a lace veil decorated with plastic pearls and a lace skirt that covers the entire plastic base. Figures 4.5". Overall height 7.25". *Courtesy of Mary Swafford. Photographed by Kylie Antolini.* $75-95.

c. 1950. If marked, not visible. Hand painted detail. Bride wears a satin skirt and carries a fabric bouquet. The base is made of food product and has a wire arch decorated with fabric flowers and a satin bow. Figures 4". Overall height 8". *Courtesy of Mary Swafford. Photographed by Kylie Antolini.* $100-120.

122

c. 1950. Not marked. Hand painted detail. Bride wears a lace skirt. 3.75". $40-55.

c. 1950. Incised "Copyrighted 1950, Coast Novelty Mfg. Co". The bride wears a net veil. The plastic base is marked "Copyrighted 1959, by Coast Novelty Mfg. Co., Venice, Calif. U.S.A." Hand painted detail. The base has an arch in the shape of a heart and is decorated with fabric flowers. Figures 4.25". Overall height 10". $75-95.

c. 1950. All figures are incised "Pfeil & Holing 1950". Hand painted features. Each groom is wearing a different military uniform. Figures 4" each. $30-45 each.

c. 1950. Incised "Copyrighted 1951, Adolph Kyer". Also stamped "Made in Germany" on the bottom. Hand painted details. I would like to know more about this mark. It is very unusual since I thought that it would be marked "West Germany" in 1951. The uniform on the sailor is old fashioned, but I believe it is an American uniform. I don't believe the collar should be all white however. I researched German uniforms and I believe I am safe in saying they never wore a white tie. Very unusual with a Cracker Jack Hat. Figures 3.25". $30-45.

c. 1940. Not marked. Hand painted detail. Bride wears a net veil. Similar to chalkware counterparts. Figures 4". *Courtesy of Mary Swafford. Photographed by Kylie Antolini*. $65-75.

c. 1940. Not marked. Hand painted detail. Bride wears a net veil. The base is food product and has a wire arch decorated with fabric flowers. Notation hand written on the bottom reads "Dan & Glad 1944". Similar to chalkware counterparts. Figures 4". Overall height 7". $95-110.

c. 1940. Not marked. Hand painted detail. Bride wears a net veil. The base is food product backed with netting and has a wire arch decorated with fabric flowers. Similar to chalkware counterparts. Figures 3.5". Overall height 7.5". *Courtesy of Mary Swafford. Photographed by Kylie Antolini*. $125-145.

c. 1950/1960. Paper label, "Made in Japan". Came in original Wilton box. Hand painted detail. Bride wears a tulle veil and skirt. Plastic base has a wire arch decorated with fabric flowers and a sugar coated bell. Figures 4.25". Overall height 10". $50-65.

c. 1960/1970. All figures marked "Made in Hong Kong". Sailors are marked with the number "513". The Marine and Air Force models are marked with the number "514". Hand painted detail. Figures 4" each. $20-30.

Ceramic

c. 1940/1950. Not marked. Hand painted detail. Figures 4.75". $50-60.

c. 1950. Incised "Copyrighted 1951". Maker's mark unreadable. Hand painted detail. Bride wears a floor length net veil. Figures 4.25". *Courtesy of Mary Swafford. Photographed by Kylie Antolini.* $60-70

c. 1940. If marked, not visible. Hand painted detail. Bride wears a net veil. The base is made of food product and has a spray of flowers decorating each side, as well as two paper American flags with 48 stars. Figures 4.75". *Courtesy of Mary Swafford. Photographed by Kylie Antolini.* $135-145.

c. 1940. If marked, not visible. Hand painted detail. Bride wears a net veil. The base is food product backed with netting and has a wire arch decorated with fabric flowers and a paper American flag with 48 stars. Figures 3.5". Overall height 8". $140-160.

c. 1940. If marked, not visible. Hand painted detail. Bride wears a net veil. Figures stand on a food product base backed with netting. Behind them is a wire arch decorated with fabric flowers and a paper American flag with 48 stars. Figures 4". Overall height 8.5". *Courtesy of Mary Swafford. Photographed by Kylie Antolini.* $140-160.

Kewpies and Cuties

It is difficult to date both the Kewpies and the cuties, because they were popular on wedding cakes from World War I through and during the World War II period, and have no distinguishing costume styles to help date them. Also, there was no export from Germany during the World War I years, and no export from either Germany or Japan during World War II. Therefore, unless I have a positive recorded date I will date most of them c. 1920-1940.

Food Product

Unknown date, possibly 1940s. Made entirely of food product with hand painted details. The bride wears a net veil. Figure 4.25". $25-35.

Unknown date, possibly 1960s. Probably American made. I have seen others that are similar, so they were apparently mass produced. They are made entirely of food product. Foil paper leaves were added for decoration. Figure 3.75". $25-35.

c. 1900. Our cover wedding couple; they are indeed cuties. The bride is stamped on her back in red, "Made in Germany" within a circle. Both dolls have hand painted details and movable legs and arms. The bride has blue glass eyes and wears a hand made bridal gown with a tulle and lace veil. She wears a fabric flower headpiece and carries a lace, satin ribbon, and fabric flower bouquet. She also wears a brown mohair wig. The groom wears a wool cutaway jacket with glass buttons and a silk undershirt and bowtie with a high paper collar. He has brown glass eyes. They came in a box with a note reading "Miniature bride and groom dressed by Doris Lancaster for G&J wedding." 5.5" each. Pair $300-350.

c. 1920. If marked, not visible. Three piece set. Hand painted features. All three dolls have movable arms. The groom has a different appearance than the bride and maid of honor. This one-of-a-kind set was dressed especially for the wedding couple. The groom wears a crepe paper suit and has painted black hair and a mustache. The bride wears a satin gown, a full lace train, and a satin headpiece with a lace veil. Her bouquet is made of satin ribbon and fabric flowers. The maid of honor is wearing pink crepe fabric with a net overdress. Her bouquet is made of dried flowers. A note came with this set stating that the set was on top of a wedding cake in 1922. It must have been a mighty huge cake. Also with the set were some favors from the wedding. Figures 6.5" each. Set $110-130.

c. 1925/1940. Probably made before WWII. Incised "Made in Japan". Hand painted details. Separate figures. Both have movable arms. Groom wears a crepe paper suit and hat. Bride wears a crepe paper gown and headpiece with an organdy veil. She carries a fabric bouquet. 3.75" each. $35-45.

c. 1920/1940. If marked, not visible. Kewpie huggers. Hand painted details. Groom wears a crepe paper hat and tux. Bride wears a crepe paper gown, chenille headpiece, and a net veil. Her bouquet is made of fabric flowers and ribbon. The figures stand on a food product base with a spray of fabric flowers on each side. Figure 3". Overall height 4.25". $70-110 (value depends on whether made in Germany or Japan).

c. 1925/1940. Probably made before WWII. If marked, not visible. Hand painted details. Separate figures. Both have movable arms. Groom wears crepe paper suit. Bride wears a satin and net gown. Figures 3.75" each. $35-45.

c. 1925/1940. Probably made before WWII. Incised "Made in Japan". Hand painted details. Separate figures. Both have movable arms. Groom wears a crepe paper suit and hat. Bride wears a ruffled organdy gown and veil with a fabric flower headpiece. She has a crepe paper flower on the front of her dress. Figures 3.25" each. $35-45.

c. 1920/1940. If marked, not visible. Kewpie huggers. Hand painted details. The groom's clothes are painted on. He wears a crepe paper hat. The bride wears an organdy skirt and a ribbon bodice. She carries a fabric flower bouquet and her veil is made of bric-a-brac and net. The base is food product and has a wire arch decorated with fabric and paper flowers and silver foil leaves. Figure 2.75". Overall height 5.25". $95-165 depending on origin.

c. 1925/1940. Probably made before WWII. If marked, not visible. Hand painted details. Separate figures. Both have movable arms. Groom wears a crepe paper suit and fabric flower boutonniere. The bride wears a crepe paper gown and a net veil. Figures 2.75" each. $25-35.

c. 1925/1940. If marked, not visible. Hand painted detail. Separate figures. Both have movable arms. The groom wears a crepe paper suit. The bride wears a crepe paper gown and a net veil with crepe paper flowers. She carries a paper ribbon bouquet. They came in a box with a sample of organdy material that was probably from the wedding gown. Figures 2.5" each. $25-35.

c. 1925/1940. Probably made before WWII. Incised "Japan". Hand painted features. Separate figures. Both have moveable arms. These appear to have never been used because of the cellophane paper still tied around their feet. Groom's suit is painted on. Bride carries a fabric flower bouquet. Figures 3" each. $15-25.

c. 1920/1940. If marked, not visible. Kewpie huggers. Hand painted features. Groom wears a crepe paper suit. Bride wears a crepe paper gown with a net veil and a chenille headpiece. Her bouquet is made of satin ribbon, and fabric flowers. The base is food product and has a wire arch decorated with fabric flowers. Figure 3.75". Overall height 6.75. $140-185, depending on origin.

c. 1925/1940. Incised "Japan". Hand painted features. Separate figures. Both have movable arms. Groom wears a painted on suit. Bride wears a crepe paper gown with fabric flowers. The figures stand on a cardboard base that has a wire arch decorated with metallic ribbon. Figures 2.75" each. Overall height 4". $45-55.

c. 1925/1940. If marked, not visible. Hand painted detail. Separate figures. Both have movable arms. Groom wears a crepe paper jacket and painted trousers. The bride wears a crepe paper gown with a satin sash and a paper flower. Figures 2.5" each. $20-30.

c. 1925/1940. Probably made before WWII. Incised "Japan". Hand painted detail. Separate figures. Both have movable arms. Groom wears a crepe paper suit. Bride wears a ruffled organdy gown and veil. She has a single crepe paper flower on her waist. They stand on a cardboard base with a step that is decorated with striped foil paper, crepe paper, and fabric flowers. There is a wire arch that is decorated with lace and organdy fabric. Figures 3.25" each. Overall height 6.5". $50-60.

c. 1925/1940. Probably made before WWII. Bride incised "Made in Japan". If groom is marked, it isn't visible. Hand painted detail. Separate figures. Both have moveable arms. Clothes for both the bride and groom are homemade and their faces do not match. One-of-a-kind set. Groom wears a satin suit. Bride wears a satin, lace, and organdy gown. Her headpiece is painted on. Bride 6.25". Groom 6.5". $45-65.

c. 1925/1940. Incised "Made in Japan". Hand painted detail. Separate figures. Both have movable arms. Groom wears a painted on suit, crepe paper hat, and a cellophane tie. The bride wears net and fabric flowers. Figures 5.25" each. $50-60.

c. 1925/1930. Probably made before WWII. In original box stamped "Made in Germany". If figures are marked, not visible. Hand painted detail. Separate figures. Both have movable arms and legs. They have never been removed from the box. Could be used for a cake topper or possibly for a doll house. Groom wears a wool suit with a satin sash. His hat is part of his molded head. The bride wears a linen gown with a ruffled collar and a linen veil with green trim and a satin bow. Bride 3.25" Groom 3.5". $60-75.

c. 1925/1930. Probably made before WWII. If marked, not visible. Made in Germany. Hand painted detail. Separate figures. Both have movable arms and legs. Could have been used for a cake topper since they came in a box with a padded silk pillow and a piece of fabric. Groom wears a wool suit with a satin sash. His hat is part of his molded head. The bride wears a long net veil and a linen gown with a ruffled collar. Groom 3.5". Bride 3.25". $55-70.

c. 1925/1940. Probably made before WWII. Incised "Germany" with some unreadable numbers. Hand painted detail. Separate figures. Bride wears a net headpiece with chenille trim. Groom 3.5". Bride 3.25". $60-80.

c. 1925/1940. Probably made before WWII. Incised "Made in Japan". Kewpie huggers. Hand painted detail. The bride wears a net veil. Base is made of food product and has a wire arch decorated with fabric flowers, a satin bow, and a silver metal bell. Figure 2". Overall height 5". $65-75.

c. 1925/1940. Probably made before WWII. Not marked. Kewpie huggers. Hand painted detail. The groom wears a painted on suit and hat, which was molded into the figure. The bride's skirt was also made into the mold. She carries a fabric flower and satin ribbon bouquet and wears a chenille headpiece and net veil. Figure 2.75". $40-60.

c. 1920/1930. Probably made before WWII. Incised "Germany". Hand painted detail. Separate figures. Groom 2.25". Bride a little over 2". $35-50.

c. 1920/1930. Probably made before WWII. Bride is incised "Germany" and the numbers "3030". No marks on groom. Separate figures. Hand painted detail. Figures. 2.5" each. $35-50.

c. 1925/1940. Probably made before WWII. Both incised "Japan". Hand painted detail. Separate figures. The figures come in a matchbox style box that was made for them. It is marked "Made in Japan" and has illustrated pictures of the figures on top. Figures 2.25" each. $20-25 with box. Without box $10-15.

c. 1925/1940. Probably made before WWII. Three piece set. Bride, groom, and minister. Bride and groom incised "Made in Japan". Minister incised "Made in Japan" with a circle and a number 3 inside. Hand painted detail. Separate figures. Bride and groom 4.75". Minister 4.25". $55-65 for set.

c. 1925/1940. Probably made before WWII. Bride stamped "Made in Japan" on feet. Hand painted detail. Separate figures. Bride 6". Groom 6.25". $30-40.

c. 1925/1940. Probably made before WWII. Both incised "Made in Jaban" (notice the upside down 'p' in Japan.) Groom is also marked "A196". Bride is also incised "A197". Hand painted detail. Separate figures. Bride 4.75". Groom 5". $25-35.

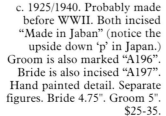

c. 1925/1940. Probably made before WWII. Bride and groom incised "Japan" on the back. Hand painted detail. Separate figures. Bride 3". Groom 3.25". $25-30.

c. 1925. Three piece set. Groom, bride, and minister. All incised "Made in Japan" and stamped "Japan" on their feet in red ink. Bride also incised "C240". Groom also incised "C241". Minister also incised "C242". Hand painted details. Figures are separate. A note came with this set stating that the bride and groom were married in 1928. Groom 4.5". Bride 4". Minister 4.5". Set $55-75.

c. 1925/1940. Probably made before WWII. Both incised "Japan" on back. Hand painted detail. Figures separate. 2" each. $10-15.

c. 1925/1940. Probably made before WWII. Not marked. Hand painted detail. Figures separate. 3.5" each. $20-30.

c. 1930. Before WWII. Kewpie huggers. Incised "Made in Japan" with two other unreadable marks below this. Hand painted detail. Groom wears a painted on suit and hat, which was molded into the figure. The bride's skirt was also made into the mold. She wears a net veil. The base is made of food product with a wire arch decorated with fabric flowers. An accompanying note states that the couple was married in Cape Cod and the wedding took place in June 1939. Figure 3". Overall height 5". $60-75.

c. 1930. If marked, not visible. Four piece set. Figures separate. Hand painted detail. Movable arms. The bride wears a crepe paper gown with a net veil. She has two crepe paper flowers in her hair and carries a crepe paper flower bouquet. The groom wears a crepe paper suit with fabric flower boutonniere. The two bridesmaids wear crepe paper gowns and hats and carry paper flower bouquets with paper lace and paper ribbon. Figures 3" each. $65-75.

Unknown date. Stamped "Made in Japan, Pioneer Merchandise Co., N.Y." in red ink. I was unable to find this company name in my research. My feeling is they are from the 1940s era. Three piece set of mice includes the bride and groom, minister, and ring bearer. Hand painted details. Bride and groom 4.5". Minister 4.5". Ring bearer 3.5". Set $50-65.

c. 1930/1940. If marked, not visible. Hand painted detail. Separate figures. Both have movable arms. Groom wears a wool suit and fabric flower boutonniere. The bride wears a satin skirt, net veil, and satin and fabric flower headpiece. Figures 5" each. $130-150.

c. 1930/1940. Groom stamped "Japan" in red ink. Bride stamped "Japan" in black ink. Hand painted detail. Separate figures. Bride 4.5". Groom 4.75". $30-40.

c. 1930/1940. If marked, not visible. Hand painted detail. Separate figures. Both have movable arms and legs. The groom wears a satin suit and hat. The bride wears a satin gown and a long net veil down her back and over her face. She also has a string of pearls around her neck and wrists. I'm sure they were homemade outfits. One-of-a-kind set. Bride 7". Groom 7.75". $60-80.

c. 1940. Soon after WWII. Groom marked "Made in Occupied Japan". Bride not marked. Hand painted detail. Separate figures. I am certain these weren't made as an original pair. However, they were probably used on a wedding cake, as a "pair", at the end of the 1940s. Bride 3.75". Groom 4". $25-35.

c. 1970. Bride has a paper label "Copyright Shackman, Made in Japan" on her feet. Hand painted detail. Figures separate. Bride's flower headband is part of the mold. Groom's hat and suit are painted. Bride 5". Groom 5.25". $40-55.

c. 1970. If marked, not visible. Molded and hand painted detail. The plastic base is unmarked and has a plastic arch decorated with fabric flowers and a set of metal rings, and satin ribbon. Figure 4". Overall height 7.5". $15-25.

c. 1925/1940. Probably made before WWII. Not marked. Hand painted detail. Figures are separate and have movable arms. Groom wears a black crepe paper suit. The bride wears a crepe paper gown with a satin ribbon sash, fabric flowers, and an organdy veil with a green chenille headband. Figures 3" each. $30-45.

c. 1925/1940. Probably made before WWII. Marked "Japan" with a star in a circle. Hand painted detail. Figures separate. Bride 4.75". Groom 5". $25-35.

c. 1925/1940. Probably made before WWII. Groom marked "Made in Japan". Hand painted detail. Figures separate and have movable arms. Bride wears a crepe gown, silk veil, and chenille headband. Figures 2.5" each. $15-20.

c. 1925/1940. Probably made before WWII. If marked, not visible. Hand painted detail. Figures separate and have movable arms. Groom wears a crepe paper suit. Bride wears a crepe paper gown and hat, with satin ribbon and fabric flowers. Figures 4" each. $25-30.

c. 1925/1940. Probably made before WWII. If marked, not visible. Hand painted detail. Figures separate and have movable arms. Bride wears a crepe paper gown and carries a bouquet of fabric flowers. Groom wears a crepe paper suit. A paper ribbon attaches both together. Figures 2.75" each. $15-20.

c. 1925/1940. Probably made before WWII. Each figure is stamped "Made in Japan" in black ink. Set comes in their original box marked "Here Comes the Bridal Pair" and "Made in Japan". Hand painted detail. Figures separate and have movable arms. Groom wears a crepe paper hat and painted suit. Bride wears a crepe paper gown with a ribbon bow and rice paper veil with bric-a-brac headband. She carries fabric flowers. Figures 4" each. With box $25-40.

c. 1925/1940. Probably made before WWII. Groom marked "Made in Japan" and a bowtie emblem. He also has a "Passed Inspection" sticker on his foot. Hand painted detail. Figures separate and have movable arms. The bride wears a silk underdress with an organdy overdress and veil. Groom's hat and suit are painted on. Figures 5" each. $45-55.

c. 1925/1940. Probably made before WWII. Both marked "Japan" with a diamond and the number 3 inside. Paper label, "Pascall" on the front. This was purchased from Australia. Hand painted detail. Figures separate and have movable arms. Groom wears crepe paper trousers and a cork hat painted white. Bride wears a net gown with chenille trim headpiece. Her bouquet is made of die cut foil flowers. They stand in a silver paper horseshoe with a metal silver bell, tied with ribbon, above their heads. Figures 3.5" each. Overall height 5.5". $50-70.

c. 1925/1940. Probably made before WWII. If marked, not visible. Hand painted detail. Figures separate and have movable arms. Groom wears a painted suit with a crepe paper hat. Bride wears a crepe paper gown and an organdy veil with bric-a-brac trim. She carries a single fabric flower. The figures stand inside a cast sugar egg and have fabric flowers at their feet. The outside of the egg is decorated with food product roses and trim, fabric flowers, and a silver paper leaf. One-of-a-kind. Figures 2.5" each. Egg stands 7" high including flowers on top. Very delicate and rare. $100-120.

c. 1930. Both have paper label, "A Reed Product, C. A. Reed Co., Williamsport, PA., Made in U.S.A." Hand painted detail. Figures separate and have movable arms. Groom wears a crepe paper suit and hat. Bride wears a crepe paper gown and net veil. She carries a crepe paper and food product bouquet and wears a black mohair wig. A note came with this set that reads "Berdella Mae Myers & Kenneth George Hall were married on 5/10/29 in Copenhagen." Figures 4.25" each. $40-55.

c. 1925/1940. Probably made before WWII. Bride marked "Made in Japan" with an unreadable mark just above. Hand painted detail. Figures separate and have movable arms. Groom wears a crepe paper suit and hat. Bride wears a crepe paper gown with a ribbon sash. She also wears a mohair wig over painted silver hair. Figures 4.5" each. $30-40.

c. 1925/1940. Probably made before WWII. Marked "Made in Japan" with a star in a circle above. Hand painted detail. Figures separate and have movable arms. Groom wears painted trousers and a silk jacket. Bride wears a crepe material gown with fabric flowers and a ribbon bouquet. She also wears a sheer linen bonnet. Both outfits appear to be homemade. Figures 7" each. $35-45.

c. 1925/1930. Probably made before WWII. Four piece set. If marked, not visible. All have hand painted celluloid facial features. Figures separate. Bodies made of pipe cleaner or chenille strips. The groom wears a crepe paper suit and satin tie. His hat is made of wool and plastic. He carries a ring in his right hand and wears a celluloid boutonniere. The bride wears a cellophane paper dress with net overdress and satin bodice, and a net and chenille veil. There are two celluloid flowers in her blond chenille hair and she carries a fabric flower bouquet with satin ribbon. The maid of honor has red chenille hair and wears a satin hat with a net veil and satin ribbon. Her gown is made of crepe paper with a net overdress and she carries a fabric flower and satin bouquet. The minister wears tiny spectacles attached to a string. His robe is made of cotton and he wears a satin tie. Figures 6" each. Set $145-165.

c. 1925/1930. Probably made before WWII. If marked, not visible. Both have hand painted celluloid facial features. Figures separate. Bodies made of pipe cleaner or chenille strips. The groom wears a crepe paper suit and satin tie. His hat is made of wool and plastic. He carries a ring in his right hand and wears a celluloid boutonniere. The bride has red chenille hair and wears a satin hat with a net veil, and satin ribbon. Her gown is made of crepe paper with a net overdress and she carries a fabric flower and satin bouquet. Figures 6" each. $60-75.

c. 1925/1930. Probably made before WWII. Three piece set. If marked, not visible. All have hand painted celluloid facial features. Figures separate. Bodies made of pipe cleaner or chenille strips. The groom wears a crepe paper suit and satin tie. His hat is made of wool and plastic. He carries a ring in his right hand and wears a celluloid boutonniere. The bride wears a cellophane paper dress with a net overdress and satin bodice, with a net and chenille veil. There are two celluloid flowers in her red chenille hair and she carries a fabric flower bouquet with satin ribbon. The maid of honor has chenille hair and wears a satin hat with a net veil and satin ribbon. Her gown is made of crepe paper with a net overdress and she carries a fabric flower and satin bouquet. A note came with this set stating that the marriage took place in August 1930. This was probably used as table decoration. Figures 6" each. $95-120.

c. 1920/1940. Not marked. Three piece set. All three have hand painted celluloid facial features. Figures separate. Bodies are made of pipe cleaner or chenille strips. The groom's jacket is made of wool. He wears a combination wood and wool hat and carries a plastic cane. The bride wears a net gown and satin ribbon sash. Her bouquet is one celluloid flower. The minister wears a silk tie and carries a bible. Bride 2.5". Groom 3.25" with hat. Minister 2.75". $50-65.

c. 1920/1940. Not marked. The box the figures came in is stamped 1947, Boston, Mass. However it is not the original box. The box was used to store them so I'm not sure if they were used in 1947 and stored at that time or if they were used earlier and someone used this later box to store them in. Figures separate. The box stored the wedding couple, a satin ribbon and sash (probably from the bride's gown), a red heart shaped felt base, and four chalkware birds. Both have hand painted celluloid facial features. Figures separate. Bodies are made of pipe cleaner or chenille strips. The groom wears a wool jacket and a wood and wool hat. His torso is wrapped with ivory satin with ink outlines and his legs are hollow plastic over pipe cleaner. He has a plastic cane in one hand and a gold ring in his right hand and wears a celluloid boutonniere. The bride wears a satin ribbon gown and a net veil with a celluloid flower headpiece. Her bouquet is made of fabric flowers in a celluloid cup. Bride 3". Groom 3.25". $40-55 (without memorabilia).

c. 1930. Probably made before WWII. Marked "Made in Japan". Hand painted detail. Figures separate and have movable arms. Bride wears a silk and lace gown with a fabric flower and ribbon bouquet, plus a fabric flower and ribbon headpiece. Both stand on painted wooden bases that are dated "Aug. 29, 1935". Figures 3.75" each. $30-40.

c. 1925/1940. Probably made before WWII. If marked, not visible. Hand painted detail. Figures separate and have movable arms. Groom wears a crepe paper suit with a silk bowtie and painted black hair. Bride wears a crepe paper dress and net veil, with a fabric flower headpiece and bouquet. Figures 6.25" each. $40-50.

c. 1925/1940. Probably made before WWII. Three piece set. All three figures stamped "Made in Japan" in black ink. Hand painted detail. The three figures are separate and have movable arms. Groom is wearing a painted suit and a crepe paper hat. Bride wears a crepe paper gown with fabric flowers and a silk veil with a chenille headband. Minister wears a crepe paper robe. Figures 2.75" each. $30-45.

c. 1925/1940. Probably made before WWII. If marked, not visible. Hand painted detail. Figures separate and have movable arms. Groom wears a crepe paper suit and hat. He has a ball and chain around his ankle. The bride wears a cotton and lace gown and matching veil, which look homemade. She carries a fabric and ribbon bouquet in one hand and a rolling pin in the other hand. Are they planning for the future? Ouch!!! Bride 4.25" (because of stiffened gown). Groom 4". One-of-a-kind set. $45-55.

c. 1930/1940. Both have paper label, "A Reed Product, C. A. Reed Co., Williamsport, PA., Made in U.S.A." Groom also has a paper label, "F.W. Woolworth Co." Hand painted detail. Figures separate and have movable arms. Groom wears a crepe paper suit and hat. Bride wears a crepe paper gown and net veil. She carries a crepe paper and food product bouquet and wears a blond mohair wig. Both figures have a food product rose on their bases. Figures 4.5" each. $40-55.

c. 1930/1940. Bottom of wooden base has paper label, "A Reed Product, C. A. Reed Co., Williamsport, PA., Made in U.S.A." Hand painted detail. Figures separate and have movable arms. Groom wears a crepe paper suit. Bride wears a crepe paper gown and headpiece. The wooden base has a wire arch that is decorated with wrapped paper, a crepe paper bell, and fabric flowers. Figures 2.5" each. Overall height 5". $35-50.

c. 1940. Bride marked "Made in USA". Hand painted detail. Figures separate and have movable arms. Groom wears a crepe paper suit. Bride wears a crepe satin dress with lace trim and carries a crepe paper flower bouquet with an organdy ribbon. Her gown appears to be home-made. Both the bride and groom have a molded composition over their originally painted hair that has again been painted (probably with the hair color of the wedding couple). The groom's facial features have been hand painted a darker color. This was probably originally a doll with female features made to look like a male (groom). One-of-a-kind set. Figures 5.5" each. $50-65.

c. 1970. Not marked. The set of three have hand painted detail. Figures separate. Each wears a synthetic hair wig. These are a pretty funny crew, but I still think they may have been used on a whimsical wedding cake. Figures 4.25" each. Set $25-35.

Composition

c. 1940. Not marked. Probably American made. Figures separate. Both have movable arms. "Patsy" style doll. Both the bride and groom have painted features. Groom is dressed in a cotton suit with a satin vest, black shoes, and a black bead tie tack. The bride wears a satin and lace gown. Figures 9" each. $120-145.

c. 1940. Not marked. Figures separate. Hand painted detail. Both dolls have braided wire for legs and arms, and cloth bodies. Both have movable parts. Hands and feet are leather. Groom wears a satin suit and wool hat. Bride wears a satin and lace gown and carries a fabric flower bouquet. She has cotton hair. Outfits handmade. One-of-a-kind set. Figures 7" each. $70-85.

c. 1920/1930. Not marked. Figures separate. Both have painted wooden heads and wire bodies. Figures separate. The groom wears a cellophane suit. The bride wears a cellophane gown and carries a crepe paper and paper ribbon bouquet. They stand on a cardboard base covered with crepe paper. The base is decorated with organdy ribbon and has a wire arch that is adorned with crepe paper flowers.. Bride 4.25". Groom 4.75". Probably one-of-a-kind. Overall height 7.25". $35-55.

c. 1950/1960. Probably handmade. Figures separate. Both have hand painted faces and wire chenille costumes. Bride carries a fabric flower and paper ribbon bouquet. 4.5" each. Probably one-of-a-kind set $15-20.

c. 1970. Handmade. Figures separate. Both are made with clothespins. Hand painted faces. The groom wears a cotton suit and a wool hat. The bride wears a cotton and lace dress, and a veil of lace and net. She has hair of yellow yarn. Bride 4". Groom 5". One-of-a-kind set. $10-15.

c. 1990. Not marked. Figures separate. Both have hand painted detail. The groom wears a fabric bow tie. The bride wears a net veil. I wanted to add these because of their unique-ness and also because they were a gift from my sister-in-law. Bride 3.25". Groom 3.5". $10-15.

c. 1940. If marked, not visible. Figures separate. Movable arms and hand painted detail. Groom wears a wool suit and has molded features and hat. The bride wears a cotton gown with lace overdress, and veil. She wears pearl beads as an accent. These both have cake residue left on their feet, so were used on a wedding cake. Bride 3". Groom 3.5". $30-40.

c. 1950. If marked, not visible. Figures separate with movable arms and hand painted details. Groom wears black wool trousers and hat, with a white fabric vest. The bride wears a satin dress with a net overdress, and veil. She has a small lace headpiece. Figures 3" each. $10-15.

c. 1940. If marked, not visible. Figures separate. Both have movable arms and hand painted detail. The groom wears a black cutaway suit with striped trousers, satin vest and tie, fabric boutonniere, and a watch chain. The bride wears a satin gown with a net veil and has an auburn mohair wig. She carries a fabric flower and a ribbon bouquet. Figures 7.5" each. $40-60.

c. 1970. Holly Hobbie. All one piece. Marked "1971, Wilton, Chicago, 60643, 301-97728, Made in Hong Kong". Figures joined at hands. Hand painted detail. The figures stand on a plastic base with a fence and arbor behind them that is decorated with fabric flowers. Figures 4.75". Overall height 7". $35-45.

c. 1970. Marked "1973, Amidan Specialties, Ogden, Utah". Also stamped "Made in USA" in black ink. Bride is on opposite side, because they have been turned around from front to back. Hand painted detail. The base is plastic with a plastic arbor and there is a pillar behind the figures. The base and arbor are decorated with fabric flowers. The pillar has a mirror and ribbon wrapped around it. Figures 4.5". Overall height 10.5". $15-25.

c.1960/1970. Marked "Copyrighted by Coast Novelty Mfg. Co., Venice, 1965". Hand painted detail. The figures sit kissing on a plastic log between three pillars with a satin covered plastic bell overhead. The plastic base is decorated with fabric flowers, organdy ribbon, and plastic beads. Figures 3.25". $15-25.

c. 1960/1970. Not marked. Hand painted detail. The plastic base has a double plastic heart in front and behind the figures. There is a lace insert on the back heart. It is decorated with fabric flowers. Figures 3". Overall height 5". $10-15.

c. 1970 to present. The bride's gown is marked "Wilton, 1316-9520, 1972 Wilton, Chicago, 60643". Hand painted detail. They are separate figures, but connect. The bride wears an organdy veil. You can just imagine the bride saying "Where do you think you're going?" as she tugs at his tails. These would be great on a groom's cake. Figures 5" each. $10-15.

c. 1970. Not marked. Hand painted detail. Bride wears a net veil. I added these because they were a gift from my husband. Figures 2.5". $5

c. 1970. Base marked "1973 Wilton Chicago, 60643, 201-206, Made in Hong Kong". Hand painted detail. The base has a double wire arch that is decorated with lace, gathered tulle, and a plastic bell. Figures 4.5". Overall height 10.5". $15-25.

c. 1970/1980. Plastic base marked "Wilton, Chicago 60643, Made in Hong Kong". Figures sit on a settee kissing. Hand painted detail. Base has a plastic arbor that is decorated with fabric flowers, tulle, and a glittered bell. Figures 4". Overall height 9". $15-25.

c. 1950. Bride stamped "Japan" with black ink. If the groom and minister are marked, it has been painted over. Three piece set. Each figure separate. Hand painted detail. Bride 4.75". Groom 5". Minister 4.5". $40-60.

c. 1950. Both separate figures have a blue paper label, "Japan". Hand painted detail. Figures 8.75" each. $30-40.

c. 1950/1960. Stamped "#N3299" in black ink. Hand painted detail. Figures 3.25" each. $15-20.

c. 1950. Incised "Josef Originals". Hand painted detail. Figure 4". $45-55. May be higher for "Josef" collectors.

c. 1950. Bride has silver foil paper label, "A Napco Ceramic, Japan", and "#S223B" stamped in black ink. The groom has "#S223A" stamped in black ink. Figures separate. Hand painted details. Figures 5.5" each. $25-40.

c. 1970/1980. If marked, not visible. These separate figures are ducks. Hand painted detail. The groom wears a felt suit and hat with a lace and satin bowtie. He also wears a fabric flower boutonniere. The bride wears an eyelet gown with a net veil, and satin ribbon. She carries a fabric flower bouquet with satin ribbon and wears a fabric flower headpiece. Figures 6.75" each. $15-25.

c. 1980/1990. Stamped "Disney Japan" in black ink. Mickey and Minnie Mouse. I added these because they are among my personal favorites. Hand painted detail. Minnie wears a dotted tulle veil with a fabric flower headpiece. Figure 5". $30-40.

c. 1930. If marked, not visible. Set of seven separate figures. Hand painted details. Crepe paper covers wire bodies. The set includes a bride, groom, minister, two bridesmaids, and two flower girls. The groom wears a crepe paper suit. The bride wears a ruffled crepe paper gown and a long tulle veil with a fabric flower headpiece. She carries a fabric flower bouquet. The two bridesmaids wear crepe paper gowns, and have fabric flowers in their hair. One flower girl carries a fabric basket with crepe paper flowers and the other carries a single fabric flower. Both wear ruffled dresses and have two fabric flowers in their hair. The minister wears crepe paper attire and carries a paper bible. My daughter, Tacey, gave this to me for Mother's Day. The set was put in a later made shadow box that I was unable to open for pictures. Bride and groom 10.5". Minister 11". Bridesmaids 9.5". Flower girls 5" and 6". $140-155 in shadow box. Without box $110-120.

c. 1940/1950. If marked, not visible. Figures separate. Hand painted details. Crepe paper covers wire body. Groom wears a crepe paper suit. Bride wears a crepe paper gown and floral bouquet, and a net veil. Figures 3.75" each. $20-30.

c. 1940. If marked, not visible. Figures separate. Hand painted details. Crepe paper covers wire body. The groom wears a crepe paper suit and hat. The bride wears a taffeta gown with a satin headpiece. She carries a crepe paper floral bouquet with satin streamers. Bride 7". Groom with hat 7.75". $35-50.

c.1930/1940. If marked, not visible. Figures separate. Hand painted details. Crepe paper covers wire body. Groom wears a crepe paper suit. Bride wears a crepe paper gown with a net overdress, and veil. She carries a crepe paper floral bouquet. Bride 10". Groom 10.5". $35-50.

c. 1950/1960. Original box marked "An Adler-Art Favor, Adler Favor and Novelty Co., St. Louis 3, Mo." Figures separate. Hand painted detail. Both have wire bodies covered with crepe paper. The groom wears a crepe paper suit with a fabric boutonniere. The bride wears a crepe paper gown with a lace overdress. She carries a fabric flower bouquet, plastic fern, and satin ribbon bouquet, and wears a mohair wig. Bride 11". Groom 11.75". $35-50.

Cherubs, Doves, Bells, and the Unusual

Some of these types of cake toppers have been used from long before the bride and groom cake top period until the present, so they are difficult to date. As with the Kewpies and cuties mentioned previously, they don't have any identifying style, like the bride and groom toppers do. Composition is therefore the main way to date these, as well as any identifying marks or dated notes that might come with the topper.

Food Product

c.1930/1950. This particular style and composition was popular into the 1950s. Marked "PAT. APL'D FOR". American made. The dove and base are made of food product. The base is backed with netting. The floral posy is made up of fabric flowers and the large dove. Very delicate. Overall height 5.5". $45-60.

Bisque

c. 1900. Not marked. Came from Scotland. These two separate cherubs probably stood proudly on top of a wedding cake in Scotland, a very long time ago. One cherub stands with two gold wedding bands in different hands (apart). The other one has two gold wedding bands interlocked (together). This possibly had a significant meaning. Figures 3.75" each. Set $100-120.

c. 1920. If marked, not visible. Probably Germany. Some hand painted gold detail with blue wings. The little cherub is at his anvil forging a gold wedding band. The base is made of food product and has an arch decorated with fabric flowers and a frosted glass ornament tied with metallic ribbon. Figure 2.5". Overall height 7". $80-100.

c. 1920. Incised with number "1196". A cherub without wings figurine. The little fellow is standing at an anvil forging a horseshoe with a large bellow behind him. Decorated with several red hearts. This particular figurine may or may not have been used as a cake topper, but figurines similar to this, with romantic allegories, would have been used. Figure 4". $30-40.

c. 1930/1940. Possibly earlier. If marked, not visible. Everything is made of food product except for the cherub, which is bisque. The cherub sits on a base and has a monolith structure behind him, plus some fabric flower sprigs. Three doves are sitting around him. There is a little hole in the cherub's hand, which probably had something in it at one time – possibly a flower. Figure 2.25". Overall height 6.5". $60-80.

c.1940. Not marked. The base, bells, flowers, and leaves are all made of a plaster mixture, or chalkware. The bells are suspended from long, paper wrapped, wire stems. The topper is decorated with netting and pearl beads for the ringers. I'm not sure if this was homemade, but if it was, it is beautifully done. Overall height 7". Very delicate. $45-60.

c. 1940. If marked, not visible. This has a light inside the bell. Hand painted detail. Bride wears a long net veil. The base is made of a cardboard cylinder decorated with satin ribbon. The base has a wire arch that is adorned with lots of netting (to hide the wires for the light), satin ribbon, bric-a-brac, fabric flowers, beads, and a plastic bell with a working light inside. The wiring for the light goes down the wire arch from the bell and through the container and is hidden within the cylinder. This topper came with napkin favors, the bride's veil and headpiece, and wedding invitations. The invitations are dated June 25, 1949. The name of the bride was Helen Anne Tolusis and the groom Harry B. Hemcher, Jr. They were married in Pittsburgh, Pennsylvania. Figure 3.25". Overall height 11". $55-70 without memorabilia. $110-120 with memorabilia.

c. 1940. Figures marked "Marblelike Novelty Company, Copyrighted 1949". This also has a light inside the bell. Hand painted detail. The base includes a satin covered cardboard cylinder with a wire arch decorated with lots of netting (to hide the wires for the light), fabric flowers, gathered satin ribbon, beading, and a plastic bell with the light inside. The wiring for the light goes down the wire arch from the bell and through the container and is hidden within the cylinder. Figure 5.5". Overall height 10.5". $85-100.

c.1940/1950. Not marked. Probably American made. The doves, base, and rings are all made of chalkware. The base is decorated with silver tinsel leaves and the rings are painted silver. Possibly used for a 25th wedding anniversary. Overall height 5.5". $35-50.

c. 1950. Figure marked "ACA 1951". Music box. Hand painted detail. The bride is dressed in a long flowing satin and lace skirt. She wears a long tulle veil and carries a fabric flower and paper ribbon bouquet. The base is made of food product with net backing and conceals a small music box within. It is decorated with a wire arch of fabric flowers, satin ribbon, and a chalkware bell. This base, depicting cherubs all around it, is one of the most elaborate I have seen. It is almost a shame that the bride's lace skirt covers the front of it. Figure 5". Overall height 12.75". $130-145.

c. 1950. Figures marked "Rainbow Doll Co. 1956". Music box. Hand painted detail. The bride wears a net veil. The cardboard cylinder base is decorated with fabric flowers, layers of satin, and net ribbon. The base also has two wire arches, one a heart that is decorated with lace and stands behind the figures. The other arch is adorned with net, satin ribbon, and a plastic bell. There is another undecorated cardboard cylinder base below the main base that conceals the music box. Between the two bases is a flat food product separator. I am not sure how all this was put onto the top of the cake. Figure 4.5". Overall height 12.25". $55-70.

c. 1940. Not marked. Doves and base are made of a very thick plastic. The base is decorated with the two doves holding silver metal rings in their beaks. There is an arch decorated with plastic leaves and fabric flowers. Overall height 7.5". $20-30.

c. 1940. Not marked. Thick plastic bell is decorated with a plastic dove, fabric flowers, and silver foil leaves. Horseshoe on the back reads "Good Luck". Overall height (with dove) 5". $25-35.

c. 1940. Not marked. Two thick plastic bells on a plastic base are decorated with two plastic doves and fabric flowers. A note attached to this topper reads "Glady's bells, for their 50th Wedding Anniversary, July 7, 1940". The names are not legible. There are two plastic horseshoes on the back with the words "Good Luck". Overall height 4.25" including dove. $25-35.

c. 1960/1970. The plastic base has a paper stamp marked "Parrish's, #8333B". Also marked "Made in Hong Kong". The base has three plastic bells covered with satin, and is decorated with pearl beads, fabric flowers, and tulle. Overall height 5.5". $10-15.

c. 1960/1970. Plastic base marked "Copyrighted by Coast Novelty Mfg. Co., Venice, Calif. U.S.A., 1965". The base is decorated with three plastic bells covered in satin, and these are attached to a center pillar. They are decorated with small glitter bells, fabric flowers, imitation pearl beads, and tulle. Overall height 8.5". $15-20.

c. 1960/1970. Plastic base marked "Wilton Woodridge, IL 60515, Hong Kong 201-4588". The base has three plastic bells covered with white glitter and is decorated with a plastic dove, tulle, and a plastic lacy heart. All are under a glass goblet. Overall height 8.25". $15-25.

c. 1960/1970. Not marked. This is probably a homemade memory jar, but it may also have been used as a cake topper. The glass jar protects the plastic flower carnation with chenille leaves (possibly the groom's boutonniere). In the top of the dome is a dove made of food product, two silver metal wedding bands, and plastic flowers with pearl centers. This is topped off with a satin ribbon and tassel. The container's outside is decorated with silver metallic paper and bric-a-brac. Overall height 10". $15-20.

c. 1960/1970. Not marked. A plastic cherub is kneeling down on a plastic bell playing his flute. The base and heart are all plastic and are decorated with fabric flowers, tulle, and satin ribbon. Figure 3". Overall height 5.5". $10-15.

Spun Cotton

c. 1960. Popular throughout 1950s to 1970s. The plastic base has two spun cotton doves with real feathers and silver metal rings in their beaks. They sit perched on top of two plastic bells covered with satin. There is a plastic pillar in back of them. Decorated with fabric flowers, satin ribbon, and netting. Overall height 7.5". $15-25.

c. 1960. Popular throughout 1950s to 1970s. Plastic base marked "Copyrighted 1959, Mfd. By Coast Novelty Mfg. Co., Venice, Calif., U.S.A." The plastic base has two spun cotton doves with real feathers, who together hold one silver metal wedding band in their beaks. There is a silver metal engagement ring sitting below them. The doves sit perched on top of two plastic bells covered with satin. Decorated with plastic beads, plastic beaded frames surrounding the edge of the bells, fabric flowers, tulle, satin ribbon, and small glittered bells. There is also a tall plastic pillar behind the doves. Overall height 9.5". $20-25.

c. 1960. Popular throughout 1950s to 1970s. Plastic base marked "KT (in circle), No. 559, Made in Hong Kong". The plastic base has two spun cotton doves with real feathers, each holding one silver metal wedding band in its beak. They sit perched on top of two plastic bells covered with satin. Decorated with plastic beads, plastic beaded frames surrounding the edge of the bells, fabric flowers, tulle, and satin ribbon. Overall height 8.5". $15-25.

Spun Glass

c. 1970. Popular from the 1960s to the present. Not marked. The glass heart stands on a glass base and has two glass doves sitting on top. Decorated with fabric flowers. Overall height 9.25". $25-35.

c. 1900. Wax clasped hands were popular from the early 1900s throughout the 1920s. One hand represents the bride's hand with an organdy and lace cuff and wearing a gold foil wedding band and bracelet. The other hand represents the groom's hand with a simple organdy cuff. The box the hands came in has a note on top that reads "Nettie and Elisa Kurson decoration wedding cake June 12, 1907". Each hand measures 4.25". Hard to find in good condition. $65-85.

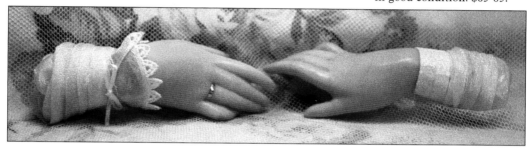

Anniversary

Porcelain

c.1940/1950. This may be chalkware with silver glaze. I wasn't sure, so I listed under porcelain. That is what it appears to be with the glaze. If marked, not visible. Figures are a shiny silver plate. The base, which is made of food product, has an arch that is decorated with fabric flowers and silver foil flowers. Figures 4". $30-40.

c. 1940/1950. If marked, not visible. Bride wears a net veil. Base is plastic coated with sugar. Overall height 4.75". $25-35.

c. 1960. Not marked. Hand painted detail. All one piece. The bottom is marked with a label, "June 5, 1912, Edna Mae Adamson, Walter Schutz, married at Columbus, Neb." They were celebrating their 50th wedding anniversary on June 5, 1962 with this bride and groom cake topper on top of their cake. "50th Anniversary" is in raised gold letters on the base. Overall height 5". $25-35.

Papier Mâché

c. 1970. Homemade. Figures are made of papier mâché and covered with lacquer or shellac. They have hand painted details. The groom sits on a chair made of wood strips. He holds a paper in his hand that reads "Happy 50th Anniversary Mr. & Mrs. Whitsy Gil." The bride stands beside him in her wedding gown. The scene is reminiscent of old wedding photographs. The marble tile base is signed "Irene Shanek 77". Well made. One-of-a-kind. Overall height 8.75". $35-45.

c. 1970. Shadow box. If marked, not visible. The box is decorated with silver foil and gold bric-a-brac. Inside, the box is padded with satin and lace. The bride and groom are standing at the bottom and there is an invitation to the anniversary celebration dated 1920-1970. A plastic bible, glittered bells, and a dove surround the invitation. The bride wears a gold painted gown. Hand painted detail. Figures 3.5". Box 7.5" by 9.5". $30-45.

c. 1960. Marked "Copyrighted 1963 by Coast Novelty Mfg. Co." Plastic base is marked "Copyrighted '59 Coast Novelty Mfg. Co., Venice, Calif. U.S.A." Hand painted detail. Bride wears a gold metallic fabric skirt and carries a beaded bouquet. Base is decorated with gold threaded tulle, fabric flowers, and gold paper foil leaves. Figures 3.75". Overall height 8". $25-35.

c. 1960/1970. If marked, not visible. Hand painted detail. Figures are encased under a glass goblet with a wooden base. The inside is decorated with dried fall flowers. The bride wears a painted gold gown. Figures 3.5". Overall height 7". $20-30.

167

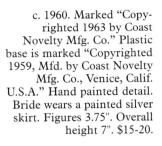

c. 1960. Marked "Copyrighted 1963 by Coast Novelty Mfg. Co." Plastic base is marked "Copyrighted 1959, Mfd. by Coast Novelty Mfg. Co., Venice, Calif. U.S.A." Hand painted detail. Bride wears a painted silver skirt. Figures 3.75". Overall height 7". $15-20.

c. 1960. Marked "Copyrighted 1963 by Coast Novelty Mfg. Co." Plastic base marked "Pedestal made in Hong Kong, 1959, Copyrighted by Coast Novelty Mfg. Co., Venice, Calif." Bride wears a silver metallic fabric skirt and beaded bouquet. Base is decorated with fabric flowers, silver threaded tulle, silver foil leaves, and a gold plastic 50th Anniversary decoration. It is strange that almost the whole topper is decorated in silver for a 50th wedding anniversary celebration. Figures 3.75". Overall height 8". $25-35.

c.1960/1970. If marked, not visible. Hand painted detail. Figures stand under a gazebo decorated with icing flowers, two plastic doves, and a gold plastic 50th Anniversary decoration. Figures 3.75". Overall height 9". $25-35.

c. 1950. Marked "A.C.A. 1950". Hand painted detail. Bride wears a painted gold gown. Figure 4.5". $25-35.

c. 1950. Marked "Copyrighted 1954, Coast Novelty Mfg. Co." Hand painted detail. All one piece. Bride wears a net veil and pearl bead necklace. Her gown is painted gold. The base is in the shape of a heart. Overall height 4". $30-40.

Food Product

c. 1930. Kewpie huggers. Came in their original box marked "Non-edible, 1 Ornament No. K2133B, Kewpie Doll Bride and Groom. Keep goods dry, Mfg. By J.N. & Co., Chicago". Figures and base are made from food product then painted. The figures are separate and have hand painted detail. The base is painted gold. The bride has a fabric headband, wears a lace shawl, and carries a bouquet of fabric flowers. The groom wears a crepe paper hat. The base is backed with netting and has a wire arch decorated with gold fabric flowers. Groom 2.75". Bride 2.5". $75-85.

c. 1950/1970. Plastic base marked "Pedestal made in Hong Kong, 1959 Copyrighted by Coast Novelty Mfg. Co., Venice, Calif." Base is decorated with fabric flowers, tulle, a sugar coated plastic bell, and a silver foil 25th Anniversary wreath. Overall height 4.75". $10-15.

c. 1960. Not marked. Came in original box marked "Perrish's Los Angeles, Calif." The base is plastic and is decorated with three golden plastic bells, fabric flowers, tulle with gold metallic thread, and several 50th Anniversary gold foil paper wreaths. Overall height 8". $15-20.

c. 1960/1970. Plastic base marked "Pedestal made in Hong Kong, 1963, Copyrighted by Coast Novelty Mfg. Co., Venice, Calif." The base is decorated with a 50th Anniversary gold foil wreath and leaves, fabric flowers, and a plastic bell. This cake topper was used on a 50th Anniversary cake for my in-laws, Ray and Ruth Henderson. Their picture, taken on June 25, 1979, stands beside their topper. Overall height 6". $10-15.

c. 1960. Plastic base marked "Copyrighted 1959, Coast Novelty Mfg. Co., Venice, CA, U.S.A." The base is decorated with three plastic bells, fabric flowers, a large plastic heart arch, three 25th Anniversary silver paper foil wreaths, and silver threaded netting. Overall height 8.75". $15-25.

c. 1960/1970. Not marked. Plastic base is decorated with fabric flowers, two plastic doves, tulle, and a gold plastic 50th Anniversary decoration. Overall height 6". $10-15.

Foreign

Clay

Unknown date. This was purchased in France by a friend and given to me as a gift for my collection. Hand painted detail. The couple appears to be in French wedding attire. Figures 3.5". $20-30.

Unknown date, probably 1970s. Made in Poland. Figures separate. Marked "Hand made Cepelia" with quite a few other Polish phrases. Hand painted detail. The wedding couple is made of wax and both are dressed in their native attire. The bride is dressed in a printed cotton dress with a lace overdress. Her hat is quite elaborate and she carries fabric flowers. The groom wears a wool coat and a red hat. Figures 5.75" each. $45-55.

c. 1990. Made in China. My husband and I purchased this little couple when we were in China. We were told by the shopkeeper that they were in their wedding costumes. Figures separate. They are made of wax and dressed in native attire. The red veil covers the bride's head so she can't be seen. Overall height 3.75". $15-25.

Unknown date. If marked, not visible. Oriental couple wearing their native wedding costume. Figures separate. Their faces are hand painted over a very thin chalk or ceramic. The bodies are made of rolled paper. The bride wears a red silk kimono with golden threads and a fabric veil. The groom wears a black robe and hat. 3.25" each. $20-30.

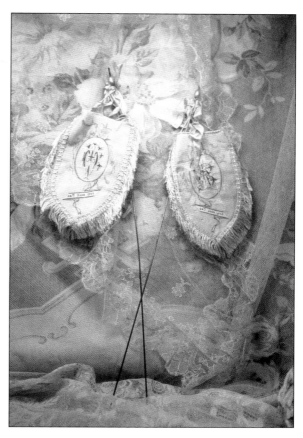

c. 1933. English Banner. This style of ornament was used on cakes instead of a cake topper for decades in the UK. This particular example is made of silk with fringe and is hand painted with the initials of the bride on one banner and the initials of the groom on the other. The date of their marriage, "28th June 1933", is on both banners. The initials, which I can't make out, are surrounded by hand painted flowers. The banners are tied to a long wire shaft by a satin ribbon. The shaft is topped with a pearl bead finial. The banners measure 5.5" by 3.5" each (without the fringe). $65-85.

Cake and Table Decorations and Party Favors

Food Product

c. 1900/1920. Not marked. At one time, this probably proudly dangled over a bride and groom on the top of a wedding cake. It might have also been used as a decoration on an elaborate cake. The word "Marriage" is molded into the pattern and painted gold. Figure 3.25". $25-35.

c. 1930/1940. Not marked. Each child plays a musical instrument. These are three examples of decoration that was popular on wedding cakes from the late 1800s to the 1940s. Figures 3.25" each. Set $25-35.

c. 1920. Possibly earlier. Actually, I believe this is parian. Not marked. Purchased from England. A good example of cake decoration that was popular on wedding cakes from the late 1800s to the 1940s. The cherub's face is part of the pillar. Figure 2.75". $30-40.

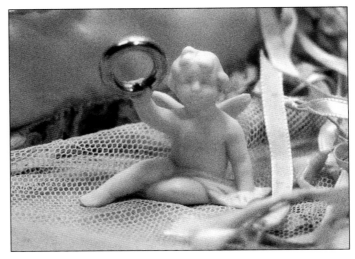

c. 1920. Possibly earlier. Not marked. Purchased from England. This cherub is sitting and holding up a gold wedding band. A good example of cake decoration that was popular on wedding cakes from the late 1800s to the 1940s. Figure 2". $30-40.

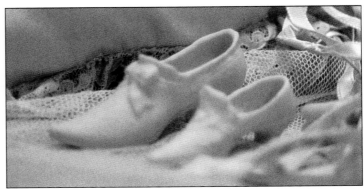

c. 1920. Not marked. Purchased from England. This cherub is sitting and holds his hand as if he is blowing a kiss. A good example of cake decoration that was popular on wedding cakes from the late 1800s to the 1940s. Figure 1.75". $25-35.

c. 1920. Not marked. Purchased from England. Shoes or slippers were a popular decoration on wedding cakes in the early part of the 1900s. The shoe means "Good Luck". The smaller one shown here has the words "Good Luck" stamped on the bottom. The shoe on the left is 2.75". $20-25. The smaller shoe on the right is 1.75". $15-20.

c. 1920. Not marked. All these examples came from England. As noted, shoes or slippers were a popular decoration on wedding cakes in the early part of the 1900s. The gold slippers are attached and measure 1.5". The single slipper with gold trim and a gold dove measures 1.75". The two gold horseshoes with white doves measure 1.25". $10-20 each.

c. 1930. Marked "Germany". Hand painted detail. It appears this little groom has all the equipment he needs to climb the ladder, fetch his bride-to-be, and elope. This might have been a decoration on a cake. Figure 2.5". $25-35.

c. 1930. Possibly earlier. Stamped "Germany" in black ink. Hand painted detail. Notice that the bride stands on the opposite side. They are quite tiny at 1". $20-25.

c. 1960. Not marked. Tiny bisque figures stand inside a porcelain bell marked "Silver 25 Anniversary". Decorated with silver beads. Overall height 1.25". $10-15.

c. 1950. Hand painted details. Salt and pepper shakers. Hand painted details. On the bottom of the bride, there is a name and date "Pat 6-11-55". On the bottom of the groom there is a name "Don". Both are written in gold lettering under glaze. Figures 3.25" each. $10-15.

c. 1950/1960. Vase. Paper label on bottom, "Ruben Originals". Hand painted detail. Figures 5". $25-35.

c. 1950/1960. Napkin rings. Marked "Japan". Hand painted gold trim. 2". Set $15-25.

c. 1950/1960. Candle holder. Marked "6822". Bride is wearing a net veil. There are two small hearts on each side of the bride and groom with a place to put small candles. Figure 2.75". $20-30.

Porcelain

c. 1950/1960. Bell. Paper label, "Leftons, Reg. U.S. PAT. OFF. Exclusives Japan". Figures sit on top of the bell ringer. 4". $20-30.

Plastic

c. 1950. Not marked. Two plastic swans used on the table for mints or nuts. Swans were and still are a very popular decoration both on the table and on the cake. The swan on the left is made of white plastic and has a painted beak and eyes. 3.5". The swan on the right is clear plastic. 3". $5-10 each.

c. 1960. Not marked. Two plastic bells decorated with paper ribbon and tulle are tied onto an engraved thank you note from the bride and groom. This was probably sitting at the guests' table as a favor. Paper is 3.5". $5.

c. 1960. Not marked. Two plastic bells sprinkled with glitter and decorated with a paper bow and fabric flowers. 2.75" each. Set $5-10.

c. 1960. Not marked. Two plastic swans coated with sugar. Swans were and still are a very popular decoration both on the table and on the cake. These swans might have been used on the cake. 2.5" each. Set $15-20.

Papier Mâché

c. 1930/1940. Not marked. Swans were and still are a very popular decoration both on the table and on the cake. This example was probably used as a table decoration. Hand painted details. 3". $25-30.

Crepe Paper

c. 1930. Not marked. Bride and groom have hand painted detail. Figures separate. Bride wears a white crepe paper gown with a long train and she carries a shredded crepe paper bouquet. The groom wears a crepe paper suit. Figures 2.5" each. $10-15.

c. 1920. Not marked. The shoe or slipper for "Good Luck". Silver paper. Possibly Dresden paper from Germany. The shoe has wax flowers tucked inside. It is a tiny 2". $20-30.

c. 1940. Homemade. Both bride and groom are separate and have pipe cleaner framework. Bride wears a crepe paper gown and a net veil with a paper cut out painted face. Groom wears a paper suit and paper cut out painted face. Figures 3.5" each. $10-15.

Celluloid

c. 1920/1930. Marked "Shimmikin Trade Mark". Hand painted detail. Four sets of bride and groom. Brides wear chenille skirts and celluloid flowers. Grooms wear a celluloid boutonniere. Figures 1.5" each. Set of four $30-40.

c. 1910. I found this example with other items dated from the 1910 period. The tiny little bride and groom have hand painted features. They may have been a wedding favor. The bride stands on the opposite side and is wearing a net veil. Figures 1.5". $10-15.

c. 1940. Not marked. Set of four separate figures. Set includes the bride, groom, and two bridesmaids. All are made of wax and cloth over wire bodies and have hand painted detail. The groom wears a fabric suit, fabric flower boutonniere, and crepe paper bowtie.
The bride wears a satin gown with a lace overdress, and a pearl necklace. She carries a bouquet of plastic flowers, and satin ribbon. The two bridesmaids wear satin gowns with a tulle overdress. They both carry plastic and fabric flowers, and tulle bouquets. The set would be too large for a wedding cake, so may have been used for table decoration. It may possibly have been used for a store display. Figures 12.75" each. Set $110-130.

Chapter Five

Wedding Cake Toppers —
Present and Future

These days, more and more brides are having their cakes made by professional confectioners. These are not just confectioners, they are truly master artists. I have spoken with a few of these professionals, and they feel that this is the trend of the future. Brides are having their wedding cakes topped with delectable sugar flowers and figures, which can be preserved as a keepsake of their wedding day. With careful preservation, such keepsakes can be handed down to future generations. It appears that this is a true renaissance revival of the nineteenth century techniques and styles. This means that someday these beautiful creations will be added to a collection, not unlike the ones we collect today.

Three wonderful confectionary artists have provided me with pictures of their spectacular creations, so I in turn can share some of these beautiful works of art with you.

What a perfect way to top the cake with these delightful figural examples by Geraldine Kidwell of Artistry in Cake of Kentucky LLC.

This formal couple is typical of the Mexican style of decorating. A plaster mold was used for the torso of the bride and face of the groom. All other body parts and clothing are hand molded from gum paste and pastillage. Features and clothing of the bridal party are copied on the figurines. The bride is approximately 7" tall and the groom is usually about an inch taller, depending on the height of the actual bride and groom. *Confection by Geraldine Kidwell. Photographed by Sam Stringer of Sam Stringer Photography.*

For the less formal wedding, the angelic innocence of this bridal pair will delight the hearts of both young and old. The substance for each figurine is a fondant blend, molded over two lollipop suckers – one for the head, the other for the body. Sitting approximately 5" from the surface of the cake and another 5" of legs dangling over the cake edge, the pair is a little large for the traditional 6" top layer and should be used on an 8". *Confection by Geraldine Kidwell. Photographed by Sam Stringer of Sam Stringer Photography.*

Appreciate the "Extraordinary Cakes for Extraordinary People" by B. Keith Ryder of BCakes by BKeith.

"When no ordinary cake will do," feast your eyes on these delicious creations by Rebecca Sutterby of Sugar Creations by Rebecca Sutterby.

Many couples look to floral posies to top their cakes. This is a floral arrangement of peach cattleya orchids, pale blue fantasy blossoms, and green foliage, all fashioned from sugar pastillage. The overall height is 7", and it's designed to fit perfectly on a top tier ranging from 6" to 8" in diameter. *Confection by B. Keith Ryder. Courtesy of B. Keith Ryder.*

This wonderful floral topper is about 4.5" in diameter and 3.5" tall. It's made up of small white roses and calla lilies, blue and lavender miniature hydrangeas, green leaves, and shimmering white butterflies all made from gumpaste (sugar dough). *Confection by Rebecca Sutterby. Courtesy of Rebecca Sutterby.*

This floral topper has the stunning appearance of spun glass. It displays beautiful yellow roses, white calla lilies, and greenery, all created from completely edible pulled sugar. The height of the topper is 6", and it can be used on a top tier ranging from 6" to 8". *Confection by B. Keith Ryder. Courtesy of B. Keith Ryder.*

This beautiful topper is one of Rebecca's personal favorites. It measures about 6" in diameter and 4" tall. It's all made of edible gumpaste and features ivory hydrangeas, periwinkle blue stephanotis, dark orange tweedia blossoms, and little orange butterflies. Rebecca says that the great thing about making sugar flowers is that you can make every one perfect, and create them in colors they aren't usually available in. *Confection by Rebecca Sutterby. Courtesy of Rebecca Sutterby.*

Chapter Six
Preservation — Old and New

It is the consensus among the confectioners/artists featured in the previous chapter that the best way to preserve a fragile new gum paste/sugar cake topper is by keeping it out of humidity and enclosing it under a dome or in a cabinet. Rebecca adds that a shadow box would be a beautiful place to display one of these creations; this keeps bugs and critters from eating it. Try to keep your topper free of dust and out of direct sunlight – if exposed to sunlight, it will become very brittle and fade. Rebecca recommends shellac to preserve your cake toppers while Geraldine uses a clear preservative spray like acrylic or varnish. Be sure the spray you use is non-yellowing. Geraldine feels that vintage confection cake toppers can be sprayed in this manner as well. Spraying the confections will keep out moisture, especially if you live in states where the humidity is high. Make sure that they are dust free before spraying, she adds.

Another thing to remember when having a floral or figural arrangement made, is to be sure the baker and/or caterer knows of your intent to preserve the arrangement. This way, the baker will make the arrangement easily removable before the cake cutting ceremony.

Other countries, such as England and Australia, commonly use gum paste and marzipan to model cake toppers that are more whimsical than those used in the United States. These will often be caricatures of the bride and groom doing things that relate to their hobbies, or dressed in outfits that represent their interests. Of course, we are seeing this style more and more these days in the United States as well, but it is more predominant in other countries.

Some artists recommend making your toppers out of a more permanent material. Besides gum paste, molding clay and cold porcelain can be used. All of the artists who have shared their creations for this book will decorate cakes to meet the individual's specifications. Your dream of a beautiful cake and the preservation of your topper as a keepsake of your wedding day can truly be achieved with the help and suggestions from these and other artists of confection.

Bibliography

Axe, John. *Kewpies Dolls and Art, Second Edition*. Grantsville, Maryland: Hobby House Press, Inc., 2001.

Axe, John. *Kewpie for Collectors*. Grantsville, Maryland: Hobby House Press, Inc., 2003.

Charsley, Simon R. *Wedding Cakes and Cultural History*, New York, New York: Routledge Publishing, 1992.

Cox, Caroline. *I Do, 100 Years of Wedding Fashion*. New York City, New York: Watson-Guptill Publications, 2000.

Fainges, Marjory. *Celluloid Dolls of the World*. Sydney, Australia: Kangaroo Press, 2000.

Herlocher, Dawn. *Doll Makers and Marks*. Norfolk, Virginia: Antique Trader Books, 1999.

Lansdell, Avril. *History in Camera, Wedding Fashions 1860-1980*. Buckinghamshire, UK: Shire Publications Ltd., 1997.

Naccarato, Vincent. *Wilton Yearbook 1979, Cake Decorating*. Woodridge, Illinois: Wilton Enterprises, Inc., 1978.

Olian, Joanne. *Wedding Fashions, 1862-1912*. New York City, New York: Dover Publications, Inc., 1994.

Queen, Sally. *The Wedding Dress, Historic Fashions Calendar Series, 2004*. Lubbock, Texas: Tech University, 2003.

Schüble, Ernest. *Cake Decoration, Cake Tops, Sides, and Ornaments*. London, England: Maclaren & Sons, Third Edition 1906.

Seeley, Mildred and Colleen. *Doll Collecting for Fun and Profit*. Tucson, Arizona: HP Books, 1983.

St. Marie, Satenig, and Carolyn Flaherty. *Romantic Victorian Weddings Then & Now*. New York, New York: Penguin Books USA Inc., 1992.

Turudich, Daniela. *Vintage Weddings, Simple Ideas for creating a Romantic Vintage Wedding*. Long Beach, California: Streamline Press, 2001.

Van Patten, Joan F. *The Collectors Encyclopedia of Nippon Porcelain Second Series*. Paducah, Kentucky: Collector Books, 1982.

White, Carole Bess. *Collectors Guide to Made in Japan Ceramics*. Paducah, Kentucky: Collector Books, 1996.

White, Carole Bess. *Collectors Guide to Made in Japan Ceramics Book II*. Paducah, Kentucky: Collector Books, 1996.

White, Carole Bess. *Collectors Guide to Made in Japan Ceramics Book III*. Paducah, Kentucky: Collector Books, 1998.

Wilton, McKinley and Norman. *The Homemakers Pictorial Encyclopedia of Modern Cake Decorating*. Chicago, Illinois: Wilton Enterprises, Inc., 1954.

Wilton. *Cake and Food Decorating Year Book by Wilton*. Chicago, Illinois: Wilton Enterprises, Inc., 1964.

Wilton, McKinley and Norman. *Pictorial Encyclopedia of Modern Cake Decorating*. Chicago, Illinois: Wilton Enterprises, Inc., 1969.

Resources

Confectioners

Artistry In Cake of Kentucky LLC
Geraldine Kidwell
452 Campbell Hill Road
Milton, Kentucky 40045
Phone: 502-268-5975
Website: www.weddingcakeskentucky.com
Email: gkidwell@iglou.com

BCakes by BKeith
B. Keith Ryder
3405 Radnor Place
Falls Church, Virginia 22042
Phone: 703-538-6222
Website: www.bcakes.com
Email: bkeith@bcakes.com

Sugar Creations by Rebecca Sutterby
Rebecca Sutterby
148 Highway 39
Savonburg, Kansas 66772
Phone: 620-754-3537
Website: www.sugarcreations.com
Email: sutterbys@ckt.net

"The Beginning"